RAYMOND JACK TYLER

RAISING DUCKS FOR MEAT

First published by Raymond Jack Tyler 2024

Copyright © 2024 by Raymond Jack Tyler

All rights reserved. No part of this publication may be reproduced, stored or transmitted in any form or by any means, electronic, mechanical, photocopying, recording, scanning, or otherwise without written permission from the publisher. It is illegal to copy this book, post it to a website, or distribute it by any other means without permission.

First edition

This book was professionally typeset on Reedsy.
Find out more at reedsy.com

Contents

1 **Chapter 1**   1
  INTRODUCTION TO RAISING DUCKS FOR MEAT   1
    Understanding The Meat Duck Industry   3
    Why Choose Ducks For Meat Production?   4
    Popular Meat Duck Breeds And Their Characteristics   6
    Overview Of Meat Duck Farming Systems   8
    Key Differences Between Duck Meat And Other Poultry Meat   11

2 **Chapter 2**   14
  SETTING UP YOUR DUCK FARM   14
    Site Selection And Farm Layout   14
    Building Duck Housing: Designs, Materials, And Features   16
    Creating The Ideal Environment: Temperature, Humidity, And Ventilation   19
    Designing Secure Enclosures To Protect Against Predators   21
    Budgeting And Initial Investments   23

3 **Chapter 3**   26
  CHOOSING THE RIGHT BREED FOR MEAT PRODUCTION   26
    Overview Of Top Meat Duck Breeds   26
    Breed-Specific Growth Rates, Meat Yields, And Flavor Profiles   28
    Considering Hybrid Vs. Purebred Ducks For Meat Production   30
    Understanding The Influence Of Breed On Market Demand And Pricing   32
    Sourcing Quality Ducklings: Choosing Reliable Hatcheries   34

4 **Chapter 4**   37
  FEEDING DUCKS FOR OPTIMAL MEAT PRODUCTION   37
    Nutritional Requirements Of Meat Ducks At Different Stages   37

    Selecting And Balancing Feed Types   39
    Feeding Schedules And Quantity Guidelines For Optimal Growth   41
    Incorporating Foraging And Grazing For Natural Diet Supplementation   43
    Cost-Effective Feeding Strategies: Reducing Waste And Maximizing Efficiency   45

5 Chapter 5   48
  HEALTH MANAGEMENT AND DISEASE PREVENTION   48
    Common Health Issues And Diseases In Meat Ducks   48
    Signs Of Illness: Early Detection And Prevention Techniques   50
    Vaccination And Parasite Management For Meat Ducks   53
    Biosecurity Practices To Prevent Disease Spread   55
    Managing Stress And Its Impact On Duck Health And Meat Quality   58

6 Chapter 6   61
  GROWTH STAGES AND MANAGING DUCKS FROM DUCKLING TO MARKET WEIGHT   61
    Brooding Young Ducklings: Setting Up A Brooding Area   61
    Caring For Ducklings: Feeding, Temperature Control, And Cleanliness   63
    Juvenile Phase: Managing Space And Feeding For Optimal Growth   65
    Preparing Ducks For Market: Diet Adjustments And Growth Monitoring   67
    Timing The Slaughter: Ideal Weight, Age, And Maturity   69

7 Chapter 7   72
  PROCESSING AND BUTCHERING TECHNIQUES   72
    Pre-Processing Preparations: Fasting And Transporting Ducks   72
    Humane Slaughtering Techniques And Considerations   74
    Plucking, Eviscerating, And Cleaning: Step-By-Step Processing Guide   76

Handling, Storing, And Packaging Duck Meat For Freshness	78
Complying With Meat Processing And Food Safety Regulations	80
8 Chapter 8	83
MARKETING AND SELLING DUCK MEAT	83
Identifying Target Markets: Restaurants, Farmers' Markets, And Direct-To-Consumer Sales	83
Developing A Brand And Marketing Strategy For Duck Meat	85
Pricing Strategies For Profitability And Competitive Advantage	87
Navigating Local And Online Sales Channels	90
Building Relationships With Customers, Retailers, And Chefs	92
9 Chapter 9	95
FINANCIAL MANAGEMENT AND PROFITABILITY	95
Calculating Startup And Operational Costs	95
Analyzing Feed, Labor, And Overhead Costs In Meat Duck Farming	98
Break-Even Analysis And Profitability Planning	100
Financial Record-Keeping And Farm Accounting Practices	102
Scaling Your Business: Expanding Flock Size And Increasing Efficiency	105
10 Chapter 10	108
SUSTAINABLE AND ETHICAL MEAT DUCK FARMING PRACTICES	108
Implementing Sustainable Feeding And Grazing Practices	108
Water Management: Reducing Waste And Ensuring Clean Water Access	110
Waste Management And Manure Use For Soil Enrichment	113
Animal Welfare And Ethical Standards For Meat Ducks	115
Incorporating Eco-Friendly Practices In Farm Operations	117

1

Chapter 1

INTRODUCTION TO RAISING DUCKS FOR MEAT

Raising ducks for meat can be a fun and profitable project. Duck meat is enjoyed around the world, prized for its rich flavor and tender texture. Lately, more people are choosing duck meat as they look to try new foods and want alternatives to chicken or turkey. Whether you're a small farmer or thinking about a larger duck farm, knowing the basics of the duck meat industry, understanding why ducks are a good choice, and learning about the best breeds and farming methods can help you succeed.

Duck farming for meat has become more popular because the demand for duck meat is rising. Today, people are interested in new culinary experiences, and duck meat brings a unique taste to their meals. It is rich in flavor and has a higher fat content than chicken, which makes it a flavorful meat that chefs and food lovers appreciate. Some restaurants include duck on their menus because it's considered a gourmet meat. This demand for duck meat provides an opportunity for farmers, as there's a growing market looking for quality duck meat.

Starting with duck farming can be easier and more flexible than other livestock ventures. Ducks don't need a lot of space compared to larger animals, and they are generally hardy and adaptable. This means they can handle different weather conditions better than some other birds. Ducks are also good at finding their own food in addition to what farmers provide, as they enjoy eating bugs and plants around them. This natural ability can help lower feeding costs and reduce the work of maintaining their diet.

Additionally, ducks grow fairly quickly. Many breeds reach market size within 8 to 12 weeks, which is shorter than some other types of livestock. This quick growth rate can lead to faster profits for farmers. Ducks are also less prone to some of the diseases that commonly affect chickens, which can make raising ducks a bit less challenging in terms of health management.

Choosing the right breed is important when raising ducks for meat. Not all ducks are equally suited for meat production, as some are better egg layers while others are better for meat. Among the popular breeds for meat are the Pekin, Muscovy, and Rouen ducks. The Pekin duck is particularly favored in the meat industry because it grows quickly, has a good size, and has tender, flavorful meat. Muscovy ducks are also popular due to their leaner meat, which some people prefer for its lower fat content. Rouen ducks, while similar in appearance to wild Mallards, grow larger and provide high-quality meat as well.

Different farming systems can be used for raising ducks. Small-scale farmers might raise their ducks on pasture, where the ducks can roam freely and forage for part of their diet. Pasture-raised ducks are often valued for their higher-quality meat, as they can eat a more varied, natural diet. Larger commercial operations may use confinement systems, where ducks are raised in barns with controlled conditions, which makes management easier and protects the ducks from predators. Both systems have their pros and cons, but each can work well depending on the size and goals of the farm.

To start a successful duck meat operation, it's helpful to understand these basic aspects of duck farming. Ducks are a hardy, adaptable option that can fit into various farm setups. Choosing the right breed and farming system will also play a big role in the success of your duck operation. With rising interest in duck meat, farmers who focus on quality and good care can enjoy a rewarding venture in the meat duck industry.

CHAPTER 1

Understanding The Meat Duck Industry

The meat duck industry has been steadily growing over the years. Although duck meat isn't as popular as chicken or pork, it has a loyal customer base that values its unique flavor and tender texture. Countries like China, France, and the United States are the biggest producers and consumers of duck meat, but many other countries also play a role in producing and exporting duck meat worldwide. This steady growth is because duck meat offers a special taste experience and can be more profitable for farmers, often selling at higher prices compared to other poultry meats like chicken and turkey.

One of the key reasons for the popularity of duck meat is its taste and texture. Duck meat has a richer, fuller flavor and is more tender than chicken. It also contains more fat, which adds to its moistness and taste, making it appealing to people looking for a more flavorful meat. Because of these qualities, duck meat is often seen as a gourmet food, and restaurants like to include it on their menus. Duck dishes are common in many types of cuisine, particularly in Chinese and French cooking, where duck meat has been used for centuries in traditional recipes. This global appeal contributes to the demand for duck meat, which can make it a profitable product for farmers to sell.

Duck farming has also become more appealing because ducks are relatively low-maintenance animals. They adapt well to various types of farming environments, making them suitable for both small farms and large commercial operations. Ducks can be raised in different systems, such as free-range or pasture-raised systems, where they roam outdoors, or in confined systems, where they are kept in barns or pens. Free-range and pasture-raised ducks are often considered to be of higher quality because they get a more natural diet, eating bugs, plants, and other foods they find outdoors. This type of farming is also popular with consumers who prefer animals raised in natural settings. Confined systems, on the other hand, are easier to manage on a large scale and protect ducks from predators and weather, which helps farmers maintain control over their ducks' environment and health.

Another reason duck farming is growing is the versatility of ducks themselves. Beyond meat, ducks provide valuable byproducts like feathers and down, which are used in other industries. Duck feathers are commonly used in items like pillows, blankets, and outdoor clothing because they provide warmth without being heavy. This additional income source can be helpful to farmers, as it adds value to each duck raised. Selling both duck meat and feathers can make duck farming more profitable and sustainable.

The growing interest in duck meat is also connected to a desire among consumers to try different types of food. People today are open to exploring flavors beyond standard chicken or beef, and duck offers a unique alternative. This interest in diverse, high-quality food options has helped the meat duck industry grow. In addition, health-conscious consumers are drawn to duck meat for its nutritional benefits, as it is a good source of protein, iron, and essential vitamins. Although duck meat is higher in fat than chicken, it also provides important nutrients that many people value in a balanced diet.

Farmers interested in duck meat production can benefit from understanding the factors driving demand and the different ways to raise ducks. Duck farming can be an economical choice, as ducks grow quickly and don't need as much land as larger livestock. In 8 to 12 weeks, most meat duck breeds reach a good market size, allowing farmers to sell their ducks sooner and see profits faster than they might with slower-growing animals. Ducks are also known for being hardy animals that resist many common poultry diseases, which helps reduce the time and money farmers need to spend on medical care.

Why Choose Ducks For Meat Production?

Raising ducks for meat can be a smart choice for several reasons. Ducks grow fast, are generally easy to care for, and can thrive in various climates and environments. Many breeds of ducks reach market weight quickly, often within 7 to 10 weeks, which makes them a fast-growing source of meat. This quick growth allows farmers to see profits sooner than they might with animals that take longer to mature. Ducks are also tough, hardy birds. They have a natural resistance to many diseases that affect other poultry, so they usually don't need as much medical care. This means you won't have to spend as much money on medications or antibiotics, making ducks a more cost-effective option.

Ducks are also low-maintenance animals compared to some other livestock. Because they are less prone to illness, they don't require specialized care or constant monitoring. Their resilience makes them a practical choice for small-scale farmers or anyone who wants to keep their farming costs down. In general, ducks can be raised with less intervention and fewer health-related expenses, which helps make duck farming easier and more affordable.

One of the main reasons ducks are a great choice for meat production is their ability to adapt to different environments. Ducks love water, and they thrive in wet or humid conditions where other types of poultry might struggle. Chickens, for example, are more sensitive to wet conditions and are prone to certain diseases when it's too damp. Ducks, on the other hand, are naturally suited to these environments and can handle rainy or muddy conditions well. This makes them a good option for farms in areas with high rainfall or damp climates.

In addition, ducks are excellent foragers. They enjoy searching for food, like bugs, small plants, and seeds, which makes them well-suited to pasture-based systems. If you have access to pasture land, ducks can help reduce the need for purchased feed because they find a lot of their own food. Ducks also help control pests, such as insects and snails, which can benefit the health of your land and reduce the need for pest control methods. Their foraging habits can help control weeds too, as they eat plants while roaming. By allowing ducks to forage on pastures, you not only save on feed costs but also improve the quality of your soil as they add natural fertilizer through their droppings. This is a win-win situation that goes beyond meat production.

Raising ducks can also contribute to biodiversity on the farm. Adding ducks to a farm with other animals, such as chickens, goats, or cows, brings variety to the livestock mix. This diversity can make your farm more sustainable and resilient. Different animals fill different roles and can even help each other. For example, ducks can control pests, which benefits other animals on the farm. A mix of animals can help create a balanced environment, which is important for the long-term health and productivity of the land. Additionally, having more than one type of animal on the farm provides multiple income sources, which can make your farming operation more stable and less dependent on a single product.

Another advantage of raising ducks is that duck meat appeals to a niche market, allowing farmers to tap into premium pricing. Duck meat is often considered a specialty product, valued for its unique taste and texture. Because of this, it can be sold at a higher price than more common meats like chicken. There is also a growing market for locally raised, sustainable, or specialty meats, and duck meat fits well in this category. People who care about where their food comes from, how it was raised, and its environmental impact are often willing to pay more for duck meat that is raised in a natural or sustainable way. By targeting these consumers, farmers can earn more per duck and create a profitable niche in the market.

Popular Meat Duck Breeds And Their Characteristics

Choosing the right breed of duck for meat production is important. Different breeds grow at different rates, have different types of meat, and even offer unique flavors. Understanding these differences can help you decide which breed will best meet your goals, whether you want a quick-growing duck, leaner meat, or a specific taste profile. Here are some of the most popular meat duck breeds and what makes each one unique.

Pekin Ducks

Pekin ducks are one of the most popular choices for meat production around the world. This breed is prized for its quick growth and high-quality meat. Pekins reach market weight in about 7 to 8 weeks, which is one of the fastest rates among meat duck breeds. This fast growth makes them ideal for commercial production, where farmers want to sell ducks quickly to make a profit sooner.

Pekin meat is known for being tender and mild in flavor. Unlike some other breeds, the flavor of Pekin duck is not very strong, which makes it appealing to many consumers who are trying duck for the first time. Because of these qualities, Pekins are the go-to breed for many duck farmers who want a reliable and popular product that sells well in both supermarkets and restaurants. Their white feathers also make them easier to pluck and clean, which is an added advantage in commercial processing.

Muscovy Ducks

Muscovy ducks are larger birds and are known for their leaner meat compared to other duck breeds. Muscovy meat has a unique flavor that is often described as more similar to beef than poultry. This makes Muscovy ducks appealing to specialty markets and customers who enjoy rich, bold flavors. Their meat has less fat than other duck breeds, which appeals to consumers looking for a healthier, leaner option.

Muscovies take a bit longer to grow, usually reaching market weight in about 10 to 12 weeks. Although they don't grow as quickly as Pekins, their unique flavor and leaner meat make them popular among chefs and customers who want something different from traditional poultry. Muscovy ducks also have a calm temperament and do well in both small and large farm environments, making them a flexible choice for different types of operations.

Rouen Ducks

Rouen ducks look similar to wild Mallards, with similar coloring, but they are larger in size. Rouens are known for their rich, flavorful meat, which has a firmer texture than that of Pekins. The taste is deeper and more complex, which makes Rouen ducks popular among consumers who enjoy gourmet or high-quality meats. Rouens take longer to reach market weight, typically around 4 to 5 months, which is much slower than Pekins or Muscovies.

While Rouens take longer to grow, their meat quality makes them worth the wait for farmers who want to provide a premium product. These ducks are often raised on smaller farms or by specialty producers who are less concerned with rapid turnover and more focused on quality and flavor. For farmers interested in selling to high-end restaurants or specialty meat markets, Rouen ducks can be a good choice.

Aylesbury Ducks

Aylesbury ducks are less common than some of the other breeds but are valued for their white feathers and high-quality meat. Similar to Pekins, Aylesbury ducks have tender meat with a mild flavor, which many consumers enjoy. Their white feathers also make them easier to pluck and clean, a quality valued in commercial production.

Aylesburys reach market weight in about 8 to 10 weeks, so they grow relatively quickly but not as fast as Pekins. They are not as widely raised as Pekins, which makes them more of a specialty option. However, for farmers who are looking for a breed that is both visually appealing and offers high-quality meat, Aylesbury ducks are worth considering. They are especially popular in regions where traditional breeds are appreciated, and there is demand for mild-flavored duck meat.

Choosing the Right Breed for Your Goals

Each of these breeds offers unique characteristics that make them suitable for different types of meat production. If your main goal is fast growth and high production, Pekins are likely the best choice due to their quick growth and mild, popular flavor. For farmers who want to cater to specialty markets with a unique flavor and leaner meat, Muscovy ducks are a great option, as their meat is distinctive and highly valued by certain consumers.

If you have a market that appreciates high-quality, rich-flavored meat, Rouen ducks can be a good fit, especially for smaller farms focused on premium products. And for those interested in a traditional duck with tender, mild meat and aesthetic appeal, Aylesbury ducks are a solid choice, offering a balance of quality and good growth rate.

When selecting a breed, think about what is most important for your business and market. Quick turnaround and mild flavor may work well for commercial settings, while lean meat or unique taste can help you reach specialty markets. Each breed brings something different, so understanding these differences will help you choose the breed that aligns best with your goals for raising ducks for meat production.

Overview Of Meat Duck Farming Systems

Ducks can be raised for meat using several different farming systems. Each system has its own benefits and challenges, so it's important to choose the one that best fits your resources, goals, and the preferences of your target market. Here, we'll look at the three main ways to raise meat ducks: free-range, pasture-raised, and confined (or intensive) systems. Each system has specific effects on the quality of the duck meat, animal welfare, costs, and the amount of land you need.

Free-Range System

In a free-range system, ducks are given lots of outdoor space to roam and explore. This method allows ducks to move freely, forage for food, and display natural behaviors, such as swimming and dabbling in water. Free-range ducks can eat plants, insects, and small animals found on the land, which can add to the quality and flavor of their meat. Many consumers prefer free-range duck meat because they believe it has better flavor and quality.

Free-range farming appeals to people who care about animal welfare, as this system provides ducks with a more natural lifestyle. The ducks have space to move around, which can reduce stress and help them stay healthy. Because of this, free-range meat often attracts consumers willing to pay more for products they see as ethically produced.

However, free-range farming has its challenges. It typically requires more land than other systems, which can make it harder to implement on a large scale. Since ducks are outside, they are more vulnerable to predators, such as foxes, raccoons, or hawks, which means you need to invest in fencing or other protections. Managing ducks in a free-range system can also be more time-consuming, as you'll need to check on them regularly and ensure they are safe. Additionally, the ducks' outdoor environment can be affected by weather, so shelter may be necessary during extreme temperatures.

Pasture-Raised System

Pasture-raised farming is similar to free-range but has some key differences. In a pasture-raised system, ducks are allowed to roam in open areas, but they are rotated through different pastures over time. This rotation helps maintain the health of the pasture, as the ducks are moved to fresh areas before they can damage the grass or soil too much. By rotating ducks to new areas, the land has time to recover and regrow, making this method more sustainable for the long term.

Pasture-raised ducks benefit from a diverse diet, as they can eat a variety of plants, insects, and other foods found in the pasture. This varied diet can enhance the flavor of the meat, giving it a rich taste that many people enjoy. For this reason, pasture-raised duck meat is often popular with sustainable and organic producers who want to offer a natural, high-quality product.

This system also supports soil health, as the ducks' droppings fertilize the land, helping plants to grow. Pasture-raised systems require land, similar to free-range, but because of the rotation, the land is better managed. Like free-range systems, though, pasture-raised farming requires more attention to protect ducks from predators and to monitor their movement across different pastures.

Confined or Intensive System

In a confined or intensive system, ducks are kept in a controlled environment, usually indoors. This system is common in large commercial operations, where many ducks are raised at once. Confined systems allow farmers to carefully control all aspects of the ducks' environment, including temperature, light, feed, and water. Because the ducks are kept indoors, they are protected from predators and weather extremes, which helps to reduce losses and maintain consistent production.

One of the main advantages of the confined system is efficiency. Ducks can be raised in large numbers, with all their needs easily met in one place. Feed, water, and waste can be managed in a way that is efficient and cost-effective. This system is popular with large-scale producers who focus on high-volume production, as it allows for close monitoring of the ducks' health and conditions. By controlling the environment, farmers can minimize disease risks and ensure that ducks grow quickly and consistently.

However, confined systems have some drawbacks. Because the ducks are kept indoors and have limited space, they are unable to roam or forage like they would in free-range or pasture-raised systems. Some consumers prefer meat from ducks that have had outdoor access, as they believe this makes for better quality and animal welfare. Intensive farming may also require more investment in buildings, ventilation, and waste management to ensure that the environment remains healthy for the ducks.

Choosing the Right System

Choosing the right system for raising meat ducks depends on several factors, including your resources, production goals, and the preferences of your market. If you're focused on producing duck meat with a strong emphasis on animal welfare and natural living conditions, free-range or pasture-raised systems may be the best choice, even though they require more land and protection against predators. If you have limited land or are focused on large-scale production, a confined system may be more efficient and manageable, though it may not appeal to consumers who prefer outdoor-raised animals.

Each system has trade-offs in terms of cost, land use, animal welfare, and management. Free-range and pasture-raised systems tend to produce meat with richer flavor and appeal to consumers interested in ethical, natural products. Confined systems, however, are designed for efficiency and control, which can make them better suited for high-volume production and more affordable prices.

Key Differences Between Duck Meat And Other Poultry Meat

Duck meat stands out from other poultry meats like chicken and turkey in several key ways. It has a darker color, higher fat content, and a richer, more intense flavor. These unique qualities make it a favorite in gourmet dishes and popular in international cuisines, such as French and Chinese cooking. Here's a closer look at what makes duck meat special and different from other poultry meats.

Color and Flavor

One of the first things you'll notice about duck meat is its color. Duck meat is darker than chicken or turkey, which is one of the reasons it has a richer, more robust flavor. The darker color is due to the way ducks use their muscles. Ducks are strong, active birds that use their wings and legs frequently, so their muscles contain more red fibers than those of chickens. These red muscle fibers give duck meat its dark color and deeper taste.

The flavor of duck meat is often described as more "gamey" than chicken. This means it has a bolder, more complex taste that some people love for its richness. Because of this unique taste, duck meat is commonly used in gourmet recipes and is a popular choice for chefs who want to create dishes with a lot of flavor. For example, French cuisine features dishes like confit de canard (duck leg slow-cooked in duck fat) and magret de canard (seared duck breast), while Chinese cuisine is famous for Peking duck, a crispy roasted duck dish.

Duck meat appeals to people who enjoy exploring different flavors and cuisines, making it a great choice for those who want to offer something unique. Many consumers appreciate the deeper, richer flavor of duck, especially those who want an alternative to the milder taste of chicken.

Higher Fat Content

Another major difference between duck and other poultry meat is its fat content. Duck meat has more fat than chicken or turkey, which adds to its flavor and texture. The fat in duck meat is considered a culinary asset, as it gives the meat a rich, savory taste. Duck fat is especially prized by chefs because it can be used to cook other foods, adding a deep flavor to roasted potatoes, vegetables, and even pastries.

The higher fat content in duck meat does mean it has more calories than chicken, but it's also worth noting that duck fat is often considered a healthier fat. Duck fat contains higher levels of monounsaturated fats, which are the same "good fats" found in olive oil. These fats can help raise healthy cholesterol levels, making duck fat a popular choice for people looking to make flavorful, heart-healthy meals.

Because of the extra fat, duck meat needs specific cooking methods. Cooking techniques like roasting or grilling help render out some of the fat, which allows it to cook evenly and keeps the meat juicy. When prepared correctly, the fat melts and flavors the meat, creating a delicious and moist dish.

Distinctive Texture

The texture of duck meat is also different from chicken or turkey. Ducks have more red muscle fibers, which makes their meat denser and less tender. This means that duck meat can be slightly tougher than chicken if not cooked properly. To bring out the best texture in duck meat, specific cooking techniques are often used. Slow roasting, braising, and even smoking are popular methods that help tenderize the meat and bring out its rich flavor.

Because of its denser texture, duck is not usually cooked in the same way as chicken or turkey. For instance, while chicken breast is often cooked quickly over high heat, duck breast is usually seared and then finished in the oven or slow-cooked for better texture and flavor. When duck meat is cooked properly, it can be tender and full of flavor, but it does require a bit more care in the kitchen.

Health Benefits and Nutritional Value

Duck meat has a few nutritional differences from chicken and turkey. For one, it is higher in iron, which can be a big benefit for health-conscious consumers, especially those looking to increase their iron intake. Iron is important for maintaining healthy blood and energy levels, so foods high in iron can be a valuable addition to the diet.

Duck meat also contains important nutrients like protein, vitamin B-6, and niacin, similar to chicken and turkey, but the higher iron and fat content give it a unique nutritional profile. Although duck meat has more fat, the nutritional benefits of duck fat and its rich flavor make it appealing to many people who want to balance taste with health.

Duck Fat in Cooking

One special aspect of duck meat is its fat, which is prized in cooking. Duck fat has a rich, savory taste and is often used as a cooking ingredient on its own. Unlike other poultry fats, duck fat has a high smoking point, which makes it ideal for frying and roasting. Chefs often use duck fat to roast potatoes, vegetables, and even meats because it adds a deep, satisfying flavor that is hard to match with other fats.

In gourmet kitchens, duck fat is considered a high-quality ingredient that enhances many dishes. It's also popular in French cooking, where it's used for dishes like confit de canard, in which duck is slow-cooked in its own fat until it becomes incredibly tender.

2

Chapter 2

SETTING UP YOUR DUCK FARM

Site Selection And Farm Layout

Choosing the right location for your duck farm is one of the most important decisions you'll make, as it can greatly affect the success of your operation. The ideal site should provide enough space for the ducks to roam, have access to clean water, and be well-drained to avoid any problems with sanitation or disease. Additionally, the farm's layout should be planned carefully to ensure the ducks are comfortable and easy to manage.

Space and Environment

When selecting a site for your duck farm, the first thing to consider is the amount of space available. Ducks need plenty of room to move around, forage, and engage in natural behaviors. If you plan to raise ducks outdoors, make sure there is enough land for them to roam freely. This space should include areas where they can find food, water, and shelter, as well as places to rest and sleep.

Another important factor is good drainage. Ducks enjoy access to water, but they do not thrive in areas where water pools and becomes stagnant. Standing water can create unhygienic conditions, leading to poor sanitation and an increased risk of diseases. Look for a location where rainwater can drain away quickly, and if the land is prone to flooding, consider raising the ground or creating drainage systems to keep the farm dry.

While ducks enjoy being near water, it's essential that the water is clean and controlled. Ducks don't like muddy puddles that can attract parasites and bacteria. You'll need a reliable, clean water source, whether it's a pond, stream, or a controlled water system with proper filtration. Ducks should have access to water for drinking, swimming, and bathing, but this water must be kept clean to prevent the spread of disease.

Accessibility

Another important factor in site selection is accessibility. You want to make sure the farm is easy to reach, especially for bringing in feed, supplies, and equipment, and for transporting ducks to the market if you plan to sell them. The location should have good road access, allowing for safe and efficient transportation. If you're buying feed or supplies from a local store, or if you plan to sell ducks or duck products, you'll want the farm to be close to major roads or transportation routes.

In addition to transportation, the farm should be close to essential utilities. This includes access to water, electricity, and possibly gas. These resources are necessary for keeping the farm running smoothly. Water is particularly important for ducks, not just for drinking, but also for cleaning their living spaces and maintaining healthy conditions. Electricity is useful for lighting, heating (if necessary), and running equipment like water pumps or automated feeders.

Farm Layout

Once you've chosen the right location, it's time to think about how to lay out the farm. A well-planned layout will make it easier to manage the ducks, improve your workflow, and reduce the amount of time you spend on daily chores.

Start by setting aside areas for housing. Ducks need shelter to protect them from the elements, particularly during extreme weather conditions. Depending on your climate, this could mean a simple barn or a more elaborate structure with proper ventilation and space for the ducks to move around.

Ducks also need space for nesting, and some breeds may require more space than others, so make sure your housing is sized appropriately.

In addition to housing, plan areas for feeding, water sources, and any other equipment you may need, such as storage for feed or tools. Having designated spaces for each function will keep the farm organized and efficient. Make sure the water sources are easy for the ducks to access, but also located away from their sleeping areas to prevent contamination.

It's also a good idea to separate the ducks based on their life stages. Ducklings, growing ducks, and market-ready ducks have different needs. For example, ducklings require a warmer, more controlled environment, while adult ducks need more space to roam. By setting up different sections of your farm for ducks at different ages, you can ensure that each group has the right conditions to thrive.

If possible, consider incorporating a rotation system for the ducks. This means moving them between different areas of the farm to prevent overgrazing and ensure that the pasture remains healthy. Rotating the ducks also helps reduce the risk of disease by limiting their exposure to contaminated areas.

Building Duck Housing: Designs, Materials, And Features

Duck housing is an important part of raising ducks, as it helps keep them safe, comfortable, and healthy. While ducks are hardy animals, they still need protection from bad weather, predators, and other risks. A well-built duck house should provide shelter while offering plenty of space, ventilation, and a comfortable environment for the ducks to thrive.

Space for Ducks to Move Around

When designing duck housing, the first thing to consider is the amount of space you need to provide for your ducks. Ducks need room to rest, nest, and move around comfortably. If ducks are crowded together in a small space, it can cause stress, lead to aggressive behavior, and make them more vulnerable to disease. As a general rule, you should allow at least 3-4 square feet of space per duck in the house. This will give them enough room to spread out and be comfortable.

If you plan to raise a large number of ducks, consider designing the housing in a modular way. A modular design means you can start with a small space and expand it as your flock grows. This flexibility makes it easier to adjust the housing as needed, without having to build a whole new structure.

Choosing the Right Materials

The materials you use to build the duck house are important for durability, safety, and comfort. Popular materials for duck housing include wood and wire mesh, but it's essential that all materials are weather-resistant and easy to clean. Ducks need a clean environment to stay healthy, so choosing materials that are simple to maintain is key.

For the flooring of the duck house, choose materials that are durable and provide proper drainage. A good floor should help keep the house dry, as damp conditions can lead to health problems like foot rot or respiratory issues. You can use concrete, wood, or plastic for the floor, but whatever you choose should be able to handle moisture and be easy to clean. Many farmers also cover the floor with straw, hay, or wood shavings. These materials provide extra comfort and help absorb moisture, keeping the ducks warmer in colder weather.

Ventilation and Temperature Control

Proper ventilation is an essential feature for duck housing. Ducks produce a lot of moisture through their breath and waste, and if the house isn't well-ventilated, this moisture can build up and cause health issues, especially respiratory problems. To prevent this, make sure the duck house has windows, vents, or other openings to allow fresh air to circulate. The air should flow freely through the house to keep the ducks comfortable and dry.

If you live in a colder climate, it's important to make sure the housing is insulated to protect the ducks from freezing temperatures. However, you don't want to seal the house too tightly, as good airflow is still necessary to avoid moisture buildup. A balance between insulation and ventilation is key to keeping ducks warm and healthy during winter months.

Protecting Ducks from Predators

Safety is another important aspect of duck housing. Ducks are vulnerable to predators such as foxes, raccoons, and birds of prey, so it's crucial to make sure the house is secure. The doors and windows should have sturdy locks or latches, and the walls and roof should be made of materials that predators can't easily get through. For added protection, you can surround the duck house with a secure, fenced enclosure to keep predators away from the ducks when they are outside.

If you're raising ducks in an area with known predators, consider using wire mesh with small openings to prevent animals from squeezing through. Also, ensure that the roof is secure and that the walls are high enough to keep out larger animals. A well-designed, predator-proof duck house will help protect your flock and give you peace of mind.

Nesting Areas and Perches

Ducks also need a place to rest and nest. While ducks can nest on the floor, some prefer to have a raised area to lay their eggs. Consider adding a perch or raised platform in the house to give them a comfortable space to nest. These nesting areas should be made of soft bedding materials like straw, hay, or wood shavings. Ducks like to have their own private space to lay eggs, so creating small, separated areas for each duck can encourage them to use the nesting spots.

If you are raising ducks for meat, providing good nesting areas is still important for their overall well-being. Nesting spots help reduce stress and allow ducks to feel safe and comfortable. It can also improve egg production if you are raising ducks for both meat and eggs.

Easy Access for Feeding and Cleaning

A well-designed duck house should also be easy for you to access. You need to be able to feed the ducks, collect eggs (if applicable), and clean the house regularly. Make sure the doors are large enough for you to easily enter and clean the space. It's also helpful to have feeding areas that are easy to refill and clean, as ducks are messy eaters. Feeding and watering systems should be designed in a way that keeps the food and water clean, preventing contamination.

CHAPTER 2

Creating The Ideal Environment: Temperature, Humidity, And Ventilation

While ducks are tough animals, they thrive in an environment that is comfortable and well-maintained. Although they are adaptable and can handle a variety of weather conditions, extreme heat, cold, or humidity can cause stress and reduce their overall health and productivity. To keep your ducks healthy and productive, it's important to control the temperature, humidity, and ventilation in their housing.

Temperature

Ducks can tolerate colder temperatures better than heat, but it's important to provide them with shelter from extreme weather. For example, in cold weather, ducks need a dry, draft-free place to sleep to stay warm. Adult ducks can handle cooler temperatures, but they should always have access to a place where they can escape the worst of the cold, especially during winter months.

For ducklings, the temperature requirements are more specific. When they are very young, they need a warmer environment to stay healthy and grow. Initially, the temperature inside their housing should be around 85°F (29°C). As the ducklings grow, you can gradually reduce the temperature by about 5°F (2.5°C) each week. By the time they are around 4 weeks old, the temperature can be closer to 70°F (21°C). This gradual reduction helps them adjust to the cooler air without stress.

Once ducks reach adulthood, they can tolerate cooler temperatures, but they still need protection from freezing conditions. Make sure the duck house provides enough insulation to keep the ducks warm during the winter months, while also offering proper ventilation to avoid moisture buildup.

Humidity

Humidity is another important factor to consider when creating the ideal environment for your ducks. Ducks naturally produce moisture through their breath and waste, so controlling the humidity levels in their housing is crucial to their health. If the humidity is too high, it can lead to an uncomfortable environment, which can cause stress, mold, and an increased risk of respiratory illnesses.

To prevent high humidity, ensure the duck house is well-ventilated to allow excess moisture to escape. If the humidity is too low, the air can become dry, which can also affect the ducks' health. This can lead to dry skin and respiratory problems. The goal is to maintain balanced humidity, keeping the environment neither too dry nor too damp.

During colder months, it's easy for the humidity to rise due to moisture from duck waste and water. To help control this, clean the housing regularly to remove waste and wet bedding, which can increase humidity. Adding dry bedding, such as straw or wood shavings, can also help absorb moisture and maintain better control over humidity levels.

Ventilation

Good ventilation is one of the most important aspects of maintaining a healthy environment for your ducks. Ducks produce a lot of moisture through their breath and waste, which can lead to damp conditions inside the house. Without proper ventilation, this moisture can build up, leading to poor air quality and respiratory problems for the ducks.

To improve ventilation, make sure there are windows, vents, or other openings in the duck house to allow fresh air to circulate. These openings should be placed strategically to ensure good airflow throughout the building. However, it's important to avoid creating strong drafts that could cause discomfort for the ducks, especially during colder months.

Adjustable vents or windows are a great feature because they allow you to control airflow and temperature based on the season. In the winter, you may want to close some vents to keep the warmth inside, while in the summer, you can open them wider to let in cool air. By adjusting the ventilation, you can help maintain a comfortable temperature and prevent moisture buildup, which can cause health issues like respiratory infections.

When considering ventilation, you should also think about the placement of the vents. They should be high enough to allow moist, warm air to escape, and low enough to allow cool, fresh air to enter. A good balance of ventilation will keep the ducks comfortable while also improving the overall air quality in the duck house.

Avoiding Drafts

While ventilation is important, it's essential to avoid strong drafts or direct cold air hitting the ducks, as this can lead to discomfort and health problems. Ducks are sensitive to drafts, and a cold, direct breeze can cause them to become chilled, which can weaken their immune system and make them more susceptible to illness.

To avoid drafts, make sure the duck house is well-insulated and that there are no large gaps where wind can blow in. Ensure that the structure is secure, with no holes or openings that could allow cold air to enter. If you live in an area with cold winters, you might want to add extra insulation or windbreaks around the duck house to keep the cold air at bay.

Designing Secure Enclosures To Protect Against Predators

Predators pose a real threat to ducks, especially if they are allowed outside in free-range or pasture-based systems. Common predators include foxes, raccoons, dogs, and birds of prey such as hawks and owls. Without proper protection, these animals can attack your ducks and cause serious harm. Therefore, building secure enclosures is essential to keeping your ducks safe.

Fencing to Keep Ducks Safe

The first step in protecting your ducks is to build a strong and secure fence around their outdoor living area. The fencing should be sturdy enough to prevent predators from breaking through. Ideally, the fence should be made from wire mesh or poultry netting, both of which are designed to keep predators out. The mesh should have a tight weave, ensuring that smaller animals, like raccoons or weasels, cannot squeeze through the gaps.

To stop predators from digging under the fence, the fencing should extend several inches into the ground. This underground extension prevents animals like foxes, dogs, or raccoons from tunneling underneath the fence and accessing the ducks. Make sure to bury the wire mesh deep enough so that predators can't easily dig through it.

In addition to the fencing around the perimeter, consider adding a roof or cover to the enclosure. This is especially important in areas where birds of prey, like hawks or eagles, are a concern. A roof will keep these birds from swooping down and attacking your ducks. It can also help keep other predators, such as stray dogs or larger animals, from getting into the enclosure from above.

Securing the Duck Housing

While the outdoor enclosure is important, it's equally essential to secure the housing where your ducks sleep and rest. The house should be designed in a way that prevents small predators from getting inside. Check all doors, windows, and ventilation openings to make sure they are tightly sealed and secured with strong latches. This will prevent raccoons, skunks, or other small animals from sneaking in during the night when the ducks are most vulnerable.

Ventilation openings are necessary to ensure good airflow inside the duck house, but these openings should be covered with mesh or wire to prevent any predators from getting through. The mesh should be fine enough to block small animals but allow for adequate airflow to keep the ducks comfortable.

If you are using a free-range or pasture-based system, you should consider additional measures to protect your ducks. One option is to use livestock guardian animals, such as dogs or llamas, which are trained to guard livestock and protect them from predators. These animals can patrol the perimeter of the farm and alert you to any potential dangers. They can also act as a deterrent to predators, making them less likely to approach your flock.

Another option is electric fencing, which can be used in addition to traditional fencing for added protection. Electric fences deliver a mild shock to animals that come into contact with them, which can discourage predators from trying to get through or over the fence. Be sure to check the local regulations about using electric fencing and make sure it's safe for your ducks and any other animals on the farm.

General Tips for Predator-Proofing

Here are some additional tips to help keep your ducks safe from predators:

• Regularly inspect your fencing and housing: Make sure there are no holes or weaknesses in the fence or duck house that predators could exploit. Repair any damage immediately to maintain a secure environment.

• Keep the area clean: Predators are often attracted to food scraps or waste. By keeping the duck enclosure clean and removing any food debris, you can reduce the likelihood of attracting unwanted visitors.

• Secure food and water: Make sure to keep food and water sources inside the protected area, especially overnight, to avoid attracting predators like raccoons or rats.

• Be mindful of the time of day: Some predators, like foxes and raccoons, are more active at night. Bring your ducks inside at night to keep them safe and prevent attacks while they are sleeping.

Budgeting And Initial Investments

Starting a duck farm requires careful planning and an understanding of the costs involved. It's important to create a clear budget to avoid unexpected financial strain as you get your farm up and running. There are several initial investments and ongoing expenses you need to consider when setting up a duck farm.

Key Initial Expenses

The first major expense you will face is the land or site rental. If you don't already own land, you'll need to rent or buy a piece of property that is suitable for raising ducks. The land should have enough space for the ducks to roam, proper drainage, and access to water.

Next, you'll need to invest in housing for your ducks. The cost of building or buying duck housing depends on the size of your farm and how many ducks you plan to raise. Duck houses must be secure, weather-resistant, and provide proper ventilation. You'll need materials like wood, wire mesh, and possibly roofing for protection from the elements. Don't forget that the housing should be big enough to give your ducks plenty of room to move around comfortably, so this expense can vary depending on your flock size.

Fencing is another essential expense, especially if you plan to allow your ducks to roam freely or use a pasture-based system. A sturdy fence, which may need to extend underground to prevent predators from digging under, is essential for keeping your ducks safe. You'll also need to invest in mesh or netting to prevent smaller predators from sneaking in.

Purchasing duck stock is another significant expense. You'll need to decide whether to buy ducklings or breed your own ducks. Buying ducklings is generally easier and faster, especially if you're just starting out. However, if you plan to raise ducks long-term, breeding your own stock may save money over time, as you won't need to purchase new ducks each season. If you choose to breed your own, you will need to invest in breeding ducks, incubators, or heat lamps to care for the eggs and young ducklings.

Ongoing Costs

Once your ducks are settled in their new home, there are several ongoing expenses to consider. The most important recurring costs are feed, water, bedding, and utilities. Ducks need a steady supply of nutritious feed to grow, and you will need to factor in the cost of purchasing feed, as well as any supplements they may require. You will also need to provide fresh, clean water for the ducks at all times, and this might involve costs related to water systems or waterers.

Bedding is another ongoing cost. You'll need to replace the bedding regularly to maintain a clean and dry living environment for your ducks. Materials like straw, wood shavings, or hay are common bedding options. Regular cleaning tools will also be needed, such as shovels, scrapers, and disinfectants.

Other ongoing costs include utilities like electricity for lighting or heating, especially if you are brooding ducklings or raising ducks in colder climates. Additionally, you may need to set aside money for emergency veterinary care or repairs for your duck housing or equipment.

Equipment Investments

In addition to the land, housing, and fencing, there are other key pieces of equipment you will need to operate a successful duck farm. You will need feeders and waterers to provide food and water to your ducks. These can vary in price depending on the size of your flock and whether you're using automatic or manual systems.

If you plan to breed your own ducks, you will need incubators to hatch eggs and possibly heat lamps to keep ducklings warm until they are old enough to join the adult flock. Keep in mind that some equipment, like incubators and waterers, might have a higher initial cost, but they can save you money in the long run by improving efficiency and productivity.

Estimating Operating Expenses

To make sure your duck farm is profitable, you will need to estimate your operating expenses. This includes calculating how much you will spend on feed, water, bedding, and utilities each month. From there, you can figure out how many ducks you need to raise to cover these costs and make a profit.

It's also important to set aside funds for emergencies. Ducks, like all animals, can fall ill or get injured, so you should have a budget for emergency vet care. In addition, there may be unexpected costs for repairs or maintenance of your farm equipment or housing.

Preparing for Future Growth

When budgeting, it's important to not only think about your current expenses but also plan for future growth. If your farm expands and you want to raise more ducks, you will need to account for additional costs for housing, feed, and equipment. Creating a budget that allows for growth will help you stay financially prepared as your duck farming operation develops.

Chapter 3

CHOOSING THE RIGHT BREED FOR MEAT PRODUCTION

Overview Of Top Meat Duck Breeds

There are several breeds of ducks commonly raised for meat production, each with its own unique characteristics. These characteristics make them suitable for different types of farming systems and market demands. Four of the most popular meat duck breeds are Pekin, Muscovy, Aylesbury, and Rouen.

Pekin Ducks

Pekin ducks are the most commonly raised breed for meat production worldwide. They are known for their fast growth, and they are typically ready to be sold at around 7 to 8 weeks of age. Pekins are large ducks, with mostly white feathers. Their meat is tender and mild in flavor, which is why it is so popular. Pekins are widely preferred in the United States and China, and they are the standard breed for duck meat production on many commercial farms. Because of their rapid growth and high demand, Pekin ducks are ideal for farmers looking to produce large quantities of duck meat in a short time.

Muscovy Ducks

Muscovy ducks are quite different from other meat ducks because they are not technically true ducks; they are more closely related to geese. Muscovies are larger and leaner than Pekins, and their meat is often described as having a rich flavor, with some people comparing it to beef or venison. Unlike Pekins, Muscovies grow more slowly, taking around 10 to 12 weeks to reach market weight. The meat they produce is darker, firmer, and has a more intense taste. This makes Muscovy ducks a favorite in gourmet cooking and specialty markets. They are particularly popular in Latin American and European cuisines, where their unique flavor is highly appreciated.

Aylesbury Ducks

Aylesbury ducks are known for their high-quality meat, which is tender and has a mild flavor. These ducks are larger and heavier than Pekins, but they take longer to mature, typically reaching market weight in 8 to 10 weeks. Aylesburys have white feathers, and their meat is known for being juicy and succulent, which is why they are a popular choice for premium markets. Though they are not raised as commonly as Pekins, Aylesburys are still highly prized, especially in the United Kingdom. They are an excellent option for farmers looking to produce a higher-end product for niche markets where the demand for high-quality duck meat is strong.

Rouen Ducks

Rouen ducks are similar in appearance to Mallards, but they are much larger. They are often considered a dual-purpose breed because they can be used both for meat and for egg production, although they are primarily raised for meat. Rouen ducks grow more slowly than Pekins, taking about 4 to 5 months to reach market weight. The meat of a Rouen duck is rich, flavorful, and darker in color than Pekin meat, which makes it appealing to consumers who prefer a stronger, more robust taste. Because of their slower growth, Rouen ducks are typically raised by farmers who are interested in producing a more traditional and flavorful product. Rouens are a great option for those looking for a slower-growing breed with a unique taste that stands out in the market.

Breed-Specific Growth Rates, Meat Yields, And Flavor Profiles

When raising ducks for meat, it's important to understand the differences between breeds in terms of growth rates, meat yields, and flavor profiles. These factors will influence how quickly you can get your ducks to market, how much meat you can expect to produce, and what kind of taste your customers will experience.

Growth Rates

The speed at which ducks grow varies depending on the breed, and this will affect how long it takes for them to reach market weight. Pekin ducks are the fastest growers. They typically reach slaughter weight in just 7 to 8 weeks. This quick growth makes Pekins a popular choice for commercial operations looking to get ducks to market quickly.

On the other hand, Muscovy ducks grow more slowly and take about 10 to 12 weeks to reach market weight. This longer growing period makes them less suitable for operations that rely on fast turnover, but their unique flavor can make them appealing for specialty markets.

Rouen ducks are another breed that takes longer to mature. They typically take around 4 to 5 months to reach market weight. While this slower growth means more time and resources, Rouens are often valued for their flavor, making them a good choice for farmers looking for a premium product with a richer taste.

Aylesbury ducks also grow slower compared to Pekins, taking about 8 to 10 weeks to reach a desirable size. While they are not as fast-growing as Pekins, Aylesburys are known for their high-quality meat, making them a good option for smaller-scale farms that focus on premium products.

Meat Yields

Meat yield is a critical factor when deciding which breed to raise. It refers to how much edible meat can be harvested from each duck. Pekin ducks are known for their excellent feed-to-meat conversion, meaning they can quickly turn feed into meat, which results in high meat yields. This makes them ideal for large-scale production, where efficiency and volume are key.

Aylesbury ducks also have high meat yields, though their slower growth rate means they produce slightly less meat than Pekins. However, Aylesburys are still considered a great option for farms looking to produce a good amount of meat, especially if they are targeting premium markets.

Muscovy ducks, while leaner than Pekins and slower to mature, still offer a solid meat yield. Their meat is leaner and less fatty, which might appeal to customers who prefer a leaner product. Although they are not as efficient as Pekins in terms of growth and meat yield, they are still a viable option, particularly for those looking for a different kind of duck meat.

Rouen ducks provide a moderate meat yield. While they may not produce as much meat as Pekins or Aylesburys, they are often raised more for their flavor than for their volume. Rouens have darker, richer meat, which makes them a good choice for farmers who want to offer a more flavorful product, even if it means a smaller yield.

Flavor Profiles

Flavor is one of the most important aspects of duck meat, and different breeds offer distinct tastes that can appeal to different consumers.

Pekin ducks have a mild, delicate flavor that is widely liked by consumers. This subtle taste makes them versatile and popular for many types of dishes. Their meat is tender and mild, which makes them suitable for a variety of cooking methods.

Muscovy ducks have a stronger, richer flavor. Their meat is often described as tasting more like beef or venison than traditional duck. This distinctive flavor makes Muscovies a great choice for specialty markets or gourmet cooking, where customers are looking for something different from the typical poultry options.

Aylesbury ducks have a flavor profile similar to Pekins, being mild and delicate, but their meat is often considered a bit more tender. This makes them a popular choice for high-end markets, where tender, flavorful meat is valued.

Rouen ducks are prized for their rich, gamey flavor, which is much more intense than that of Pekin ducks. Consumers who enjoy a more robust, distinctive taste will appreciate Rouen ducks. Their darker meat has a stronger flavor, which is ideal for those seeking a more unique and hearty taste.

Considering Hybrid Vs. Purebred Ducks For Meat Production

When deciding which ducks to raise for meat production, one important choice is whether to use hybrid ducks or purebred ducks. Each type has its own advantages and challenges, so your decision will depend on the goals of your farm and the market you're aiming for.

Hybrid Ducks

Hybrid ducks are the result of crossbreeding two different purebred strains. The purpose of this crossbreeding is to combine desirable traits, such as fast growth, high meat yield, and better disease resistance. Hybrid ducks are often bred for performance, and their main strength is their efficiency.

For example, hybrids can grow very quickly and convert feed into meat more effectively than purebreds. This makes them ideal for large-scale commercial operations where the focus is on maximizing production and minimizing costs. In large operations, speed and volume are important, and hybrid ducks are perfect for this purpose. These ducks can reach market weight in a shorter amount of time, which means farmers can sell more meat in less time. This efficiency is a key reason why hybrid ducks, like the Cornish-X variety used in chicken production, are common in many commercial poultry farms.

Hybrid ducks are also known for their hardiness and resistance to diseases. This makes them easier to manage since they typically require less veterinary care and fewer medications. The focus on growth and meat yield, along with their resistance to common diseases, makes hybrid ducks ideal for farmers who are looking for cost-effective solutions and a steady supply of high-quality meat.

However, there are some downsides. While hybrid ducks are great for commercial production, they may not have the unique characteristics that purebred ducks offer, such as distinct flavors or heritage traits. As a result, they may not be as appealing to consumers who are looking for specialty or gourmet products. Additionally, hybrids may not be able to breed true-to-type, meaning that if you try to breed them, the offspring may not have the same desirable traits as the parents. This makes it difficult for farmers to save breeding stock and continue production from their own flock.

Purebred Ducks

Purebred ducks, on the other hand, are distinct breeds that have been carefully bred over generations to maintain their unique characteristics. These breeds are often prized for specific traits, such as flavor, size, or appearance. Unlike hybrids, purebred ducks are maintained for their traditional qualities and are often raised for smaller-scale, niche markets.

The downside to purebred ducks is that they tend to grow slower than hybrid ducks and may not produce as much meat. They often require more time to reach market weight, which can make them less efficient in terms of meat production. This slower growth means that farmers may need to invest more in feed and care over a longer period before they can sell the ducks.

However, purebred ducks have their own advantages. For example, breeds like the Aylesbury, Muscovy, and Rouen are highly valued for their unique flavors and textures. Consumers who are looking for more distinct and gourmet products may be willing to pay a premium for these ducks. Farmers who are focused on creating high-quality, specialty meat may find that purebred ducks are a better choice, as they can charge higher prices for meat that is considered a delicacy.

Purebred ducks also offer the benefit of being able to breed true-to-type. This means that farmers can save breeding stock from their own flock and use them to produce more ducks with the same desirable characteristics. For small-scale farmers or those involved in sustainable farming practices, the ability to breed purebred ducks is an attractive feature that helps maintain long-term production without relying on purchasing new stock.

In addition, purebred ducks are often more suited for traditional or organic farming systems. These breeds may be more adaptable to outdoor environments or specific farming practices, such as free-range or pasture-raised systems, which can appeal to customers who prioritize sustainability, animal welfare, and locally sourced food.

Hybrid vs. Purebred: Which is Best for You?

Choosing between hybrid and purebred ducks depends on the type of operation you want to run. If your goal is to produce large quantities of duck meat quickly and at a low cost, hybrid ducks are likely the best choice. They grow faster, have higher meat yields, and are easier to manage in large-scale operations. Hybrid ducks are perfect for commercial farms where speed and efficiency are key.

However, if you're focused on quality over quantity and are targeting a niche market that values flavor and heritage breeds, then purebred ducks might be a better option. These ducks may take longer to grow, but they offer unique qualities that can be sold at premium prices, especially if you're aiming at gourmet or specialty markets. Purebred ducks also allow for breeding your own stock, which can reduce long-term costs and help you maintain control over the characteristics of your flock.

Understanding The Influence Of Breed On Market Demand And Pricing

The breed of duck you choose to raise plays an important role in determining how much demand there will be for your meat and how much you can charge for it. Different breeds of ducks have different characteristics that affect both their appeal to consumers and their market price. Some breeds are in high demand because they grow quickly and have mild flavors, while others are more popular in niche markets where people are willing to pay more for unique tastes or traditional methods of farming.

Popular Breeds: Pekin Ducks

Pekin ducks are one of the most widely raised meat duck breeds. They are well-known for their fast growth and mild flavor. Pekin ducks typically reach market weight in 7-8 weeks, which makes them ideal for large-scale commercial farming. Because they grow quickly and have a meat that appeals to a broad range of consumers, Pekins can be sold at competitive prices, making them a popular choice in bigger markets.

The high demand for Pekin ducks in commercial markets means they are often produced in large quantities. These ducks are sold in supermarkets and restaurants, where consumers may be looking for affordable, easy-to-prepare meat. Pekins are a great choice for farmers aiming to meet the needs of these larger, mainstream markets because they produce a lot of meat in a short amount of time, helping farmers keep production costs down.

However, because Pekins are in such high supply, they are also subject to price competition, and farmers may find that the price they can charge is lower than for specialty breeds. So, while Pekin ducks can generate steady sales, they may not bring in as much profit per bird as some of the rarer or slower-growing breeds.

Premium and Niche Breeds: Muscovy, Aylesbury, and Rouen Ducks

On the other hand, breeds like Muscovy, Aylesbury, and Rouen are often raised for niche markets. These breeds are not as common as Pekins, but they are highly valued for their unique flavors, textures, and slower-growing, traditional characteristics. As a result, they can often be sold at higher prices, especially in gourmet food markets, local farmers' markets, or specialty butcher shops.

Muscovy ducks, for example, have a distinct flavor that some people compare to beef or venison. This unique taste appeals to gourmet chefs and food enthusiasts, especially in Latin American and European cuisines. Because they are less common and take longer to mature (about 10-12 weeks), Muscovies can command a higher price. They may not be as widely available as Pekins, which increases their value in specialty markets.

Aylesbury ducks are another breed with a reputation for high-quality meat. These ducks are known for their tender, mild-flavored meat and are often considered a premium product in the United Kingdom. Aylesburys take longer to grow (around 8-10 weeks), but their meat is prized for its texture and flavor, making them a good option for farmers focusing on more upscale, gourmet consumers who are willing to pay more for quality.

Rouen ducks are similar in appearance to Mallards but much larger. They are valued for their rich, gamey flavor and are often sought after by consumers who prefer darker, more intense-tasting meat. Rouen ducks are slower to mature than Pekins, taking around 4-5 months to reach market weight, but they are highly regarded for their flavor. This makes them a great option for farmers who want to cater to a more specialized market, such as those interested in traditional, slow-growing breeds or those seeking meat with a distinctive taste.

Market Demand and Pricing

The demand for duck meat and the prices you can charge depend largely on the breed you raise. If your focus is on large-scale commercial markets, you'll likely want to choose a breed like Pekin, which grows quickly and offers a mild flavor that appeals to a wide audience. Pekin ducks can be sold at competitive prices in supermarkets and restaurants, and their fast growth means you can produce a lot of meat in a short amount of time.

If you are targeting a niche market, such as gourmet food lovers or consumers who value traditional farming methods, breeds like Muscovy, Aylesbury, and Rouen may be more profitable. These breeds may take longer to grow, but their unique flavors, textures, and slower production times often allow farmers to charge higher prices. Consumers in these markets are often looking for high-quality, specialty meats and are willing to pay a premium for the distinctive qualities offered by these breeds.

Making the Right Choice for Your Farm

To determine the best breed for your farm, it's important to understand the type of market you want to serve. If you're aiming to produce a large volume of duck meat quickly and cost-effectively, Pekin ducks may be the best choice. They offer fast growth, high meat yield, and steady demand in commercial markets.

However, if you're looking to target a more specific, higher-end market, you may find that Muscovy, Aylesbury, or Rouen ducks can provide better profit margins due to their unique flavors and slower growth rates. These breeds may not grow as quickly as Pekins, but their meat can be sold at a premium to consumers seeking quality over quantity.

Sourcing Quality Ducklings: Choosing Reliable Hatcheries

After deciding which breed of ducks you want to raise, the next important step is to find healthy and high-quality ducklings. Sourcing ducklings from a reliable hatchery is essential to ensure you get strong, healthy birds that will grow well and produce good meat. The quality of the ducklings you start with will have a direct impact on your farming success, so it's important to take your time and choose the right hatchery.

Choosing a Reliable Hatchery

When looking for a hatchery to buy your ducklings, it's crucial to find one with a good reputation for providing healthy, well-bred birds. Research hatcheries online or ask for recommendations from other duck farmers. A reputable hatchery should be known for breeding ducks that are healthy, robust, and genetically strong. The hatchery should also be willing to answer any questions you have about the breed, care, or raising ducks in general.

The health of your ducklings is the most important factor. Healthy ducklings will have a higher chance of growing into strong, productive ducks. A good hatchery will ensure their ducklings are disease-free and well cared for before shipping them. It's always a good idea to visit the hatchery in person, if possible, to see the conditions where the ducks are raised. You want to be sure they are well taken care of, as this will directly affect the health and well-being of the ducklings you receive.

Biosecurity Practices

One of the most important things to consider when choosing a hatchery is their biosecurity practices. Biosecurity refers to the steps taken to prevent the spread of diseases between birds. A good hatchery will have strict biosecurity measures in place to ensure their ducks are kept healthy and disease-free. This includes things like keeping ducks in clean, well-maintained facilities, monitoring the health of their flock, and implementing practices to prevent any disease from entering or spreading.

Ask the hatchery about their biosecurity practices before you make a purchase. Find out what kind of health checks they do on their birds, how they manage the cleanliness of their facilities, and what steps they take to prevent diseases like avian flu or other common poultry illnesses. This is important because introducing sick or diseased birds to your farm can lead to serious health issues in your entire flock, which can be costly and damaging to your business.

Breeding Practices and Health Standards

In addition to biosecurity, you should ask about the hatchery's breeding practices. Reliable hatcheries will provide information about the breeding stock they use and how they ensure the genetic quality of their birds. For example, they might select ducks with desirable traits, such as good meat production, disease resistance, or fast growth rates. Knowing the quality of the breeding stock gives you confidence that you are getting good ducklings that will meet your farming goals.

If you are new to raising ducks, it's also helpful to choose a hatchery that provides care instructions and guidance on how to raise your ducklings properly. Many hatcheries will offer advice on feeding, watering, housing, and general care to help ensure your ducklings grow into healthy adult ducks. Some hatcheries even provide growth rate expectations, which can help you plan your farm's production timeline.

Customer Support

Another factor to consider when choosing a hatchery is the level of customer support they offer. A reliable hatchery should be available to answer any questions you have about your ducklings or their care. They should be able to provide guidance if you run into problems or need help with specific issues, such as illness, growth, or behavior problems in your ducks. Good customer support can save you time, money, and stress, especially when you're just starting out.

Considerations for New Farmers

If you are a beginner in duck farming, it may be helpful to choose a hatchery that specializes in providing starter flocks or offering educational resources for new farmers. Some hatcheries offer packages that include a mix of breeds or the number of ducklings you need to start your farm, along with the necessary guidance to help you succeed.

In addition to purchasing healthy ducklings, you may also need to consider the cost. While it's important to find a hatchery with healthy birds, you should also make sure the cost of the ducklings fits within your budget. Keep in mind that while buying cheaper ducklings may save money upfront, it could end up being more expensive in the long run if the birds are unhealthy or do not grow well.

4

Chapter 4

FEEDING DUCKS FOR OPTIMAL MEAT PRODUCTION

Nutritional Requirements Of Meat Ducks At Different Stages

Ducks, like all animals, have different nutritional needs depending on their age and stage of growth. Understanding these needs is important to ensure that your ducks grow healthy, strong, and produce high-quality meat. Proper nutrition at each stage of their life helps support their growth, muscle development, and overall health.

Ducklings (0-4 Weeks)

When ducks are first born, they are in a rapid growth phase and need a high-protein diet to support their development. Ducklings, from birth until around 4 weeks old, require a specially formulated starter feed that is rich in protein—typically about 18-20%. This high protein content helps them build strong muscles and bones. Protein is also important for their immune system, ensuring that the ducklings stay healthy as they grow.

In addition to protein, ducklings need a variety of vitamins and minerals, especially calcium and phosphorus. These minerals are essential for bone growth and skeletal health. Without the proper levels of calcium and phosphorus, ducklings may develop weak bones, which can affect their growth and overall health. At this early stage, ducklings also need a balance of fats in their diet for energy, which fuels their rapid growth.

Water is just as important as food during this stage. Ducklings need constant access to clean, fresh water to help them digest their food and stay hydrated, which is essential for their growth.

Growers (4-8 Weeks)

As ducks grow and approach the next stage of life, their nutritional needs change. From about 4 to 8 weeks, ducks are known as growers, and their growth rate starts to slow down slightly. During this stage, they still need a high-quality diet to continue growing, but their protein requirements are lower than when they were ducklings. A grower feed with about 16-18% protein is ideal for this stage. This reduced protein level helps the ducks gain healthy weight without encouraging excess fat buildup.

While protein is still important, ducks at this stage also need a good balance of other nutrients to support muscle development, healthy weight gain, and overall health. Carbohydrates become more important for energy, as ducks in this phase are active and need extra calories to fuel their growth. Fats also remain essential for energy, but they should be provided in moderation to prevent the ducks from becoming too fatty. Essential minerals like zinc and selenium are important for their immune system, muscle function, and overall health. These nutrients help the ducks grow efficiently and stay strong.

As ducks approach market size, it's important to gradually transition from the high-protein starter feed to the grower feed. This transition should be done slowly to ensure that the ducks are adjusting properly to the change in their diet.

Finisher (8 Weeks to Market)

Once ducks reach the finisher phase, which is from 8 weeks until they are ready for market, their growth slows even more. This is the stage where ducks put on most of their weight. The goal during this phase is to maintain steady growth without the ducks becoming too fatty. To achieve this, the protein content of their feed should be reduced to around 14-16%. This allows ducks to continue gaining weight without putting on excess fat. At this stage, the focus is on providing enough energy to maintain healthy growth.

A well-balanced finisher feed is important at this stage to ensure that ducks reach market weight efficiently. The feed should provide the right balance of fats, carbohydrates, and proteins to support steady weight gain. While protein is still necessary for muscle development, reducing protein levels in the feed helps prevent ducks from becoming overly fatty. Finisher feed should also contain enough vitamins and minerals to keep the ducks healthy, especially vitamin A, vitamin D, and calcium, which are important for overall health and bone strength.

Selecting And Balancing Feed Types

When raising ducks, one of the most important things you'll need to consider is what to feed them. The right combination of feed will depend on your farming system, your budget, and your goals for the ducks' health and growth. Ducks can be fed a mix of grains, pelleted feeds, and natural feed, each offering different benefits.

Grains

Grains such as corn, barley, oats, and wheat are common ingredients in duck diets. These grains provide a good source of energy, which is essential for ducks to grow strong and stay healthy. Corn is particularly high in carbohydrates, making it a great energy source for ducks, especially during periods of rapid growth. However, while corn is useful, it should be balanced with other grains to avoid an overly starchy diet, which can cause digestive issues.

In addition to corn, barley, oats, and wheat are also important grains to include in your ducks' diet. These grains offer a variety of nutrients, including fiber and other vitamins, which help with digestion and overall health. Grains can be fed either as a mixture or included in specially formulated feeds. When feeding grains, it's important to make sure they are not the only food source, as ducks also need proteins, vitamins, and minerals for optimal growth.

Grains can also be an affordable way to provide energy for your ducks, especially if you have access to local sources. They can be used as part of a balanced diet, but should always be complemented with other feed types to ensure that your ducks receive all of the necessary nutrients.

Pellets

Pelleted feed is a popular and convenient option for feeding ducks. This type of feed is specially formulated to meet the nutritional needs of ducks at various stages of their life, from ducklings to adults. Pellets are made by compressing a mixture of ingredients into small, easy-to-eat shapes, making it simpler for ducks to consume and digest. Because the feed is balanced and already formulated with the right levels of nutrients, pelleted feed can ensure that ducks are getting a consistent, complete diet.

One of the key advantages of pelleted feed is its efficiency. Ducks tend to eat pellets quickly and efficiently, so there is less waste compared to loose grains or other types of feed. The balanced mix in the pellets often includes grains, protein, vitamins, and minerals, making it an all-in-one solution for feeding your ducks. Pellets are available in different formulas depending on the ducks' age and nutritional needs, which helps support healthy growth and development.

For example, starter pellets for young ducklings contain higher levels of protein and energy to support their fast growth, while grower and finisher pellets for older ducks have a lower protein content to help maintain steady growth without excess fat.

Pelleted feed is a good option for duck farms where ease of feeding and consistency is important. However, it may be more expensive than using grains alone, especially if you have a large number of ducks to feed.

Natural Feed

If you are raising ducks in a free-range or pasture-based system, they can also be fed a variety of natural foods. Ducks are natural foragers, which means they love to search for plants, insects, and other food items. Some of the most common types of natural feed include fresh grasses, weeds, and seeds. Ducks can graze on a variety of plants, which gives them extra nutrients, especially fiber, which aids in digestion.

Allowing ducks to forage naturally can also improve the diversity of their diet, which can be beneficial for their health. However, while natural feed like plants and insects is a great supplement, it should not be the only source of food. Natural feed may lack certain essential nutrients such as protein and vitamins, so it's important to supplement it with grains and pellets to make sure the ducks get all the nutrients they need.

Using natural feed can be more cost-effective if you have access to plenty of pasture or land for your ducks to forage. It can also improve the flavor of the duck meat, as ducks that have access to a varied diet often produce richer, more flavorful meat. However, it's essential to monitor their diet carefully to ensure they are getting a balanced intake of all the necessary nutrients.

Balancing Feed Types

For the best results, it's important to balance these different feed types. Grains, pellets, and natural feed all have their benefits, but they should be used together to provide a well-rounded diet for your ducks. A diet that is too high in grains, for example, might lack the necessary protein or minerals, while relying too much on natural feed could result in nutrient deficiencies.

For ducks that are growing quickly or approaching market weight, it's especially important to make sure they have access to a complete diet. Pellets are often the most reliable way to ensure balanced nutrition, but supplementing with grains and natural feed can help keep the ducks happy and healthy.

Feeding Schedules And Quantity Guidelines For Optimal Growth

Having a proper feeding schedule is important to ensure your ducks grow well and stay healthy. Ducks need consistent nutrition to support their growth and development, and knowing how much and when to feed them can help prevent issues like obesity and poor meat quality. While some farmers prefer to feed ducks twice a day, others choose free-choice feeding, where the ducks can access food all day. However, no matter the feeding method, it's important to avoid overfeeding, as this can lead to unhealthy weight gain, which affects both the ducks' health and the quality of their meat.

Feeding Ducklings (0-4 Weeks)

Ducklings grow quickly, so they need the right amount of feed during their first few weeks. During this stage, you should feed them starter feed, which is specially made to support their fast growth. Ducklings typically need around 1.5-2 pounds of feed per week for every 10 ducklings. This feed is high in protein, which helps ducklings develop strong muscles and bones. As the ducklings grow, you should continue to offer the starter feed, but be careful not to give them too much, as rapid weight gain can lead to fatty meat later on.

It's important to monitor the ducklings' health and growth. If you notice that they're gaining weight too quickly or seem sluggish, it may be a sign they're being overfed. On the other hand, if they aren't growing at the right rate, you may need to increase their feed slightly.

Feeding Growers (4-8 Weeks)

As ducks grow older, their nutritional needs change. During the grower phase, which is typically between 4-8 weeks, ducks begin to eat more and their feed intake will increase. You can reduce the protein content of their feed slightly, but it should still support healthy muscle development and weight gain. During this stage, feed consumption will increase to about 3-4 pounds per duck each week. This is a time of steady growth, so make sure the ducks are gaining weight at a healthy rate.

Keep an eye on their condition and weight. If the ducks appear to be growing too fast, you can slightly reduce their feed to avoid excessive fat buildup. Alternatively, if their growth seems slower than expected, you may need to increase their feed amount or ensure they are getting enough nutrients.

Feeding Finishers (8 Weeks to Market)

Once ducks reach the finisher stage, usually around 8 weeks of age or when they are getting closer to market weight, their feed intake increases further. At this stage, ducks are focused on putting on weight, and the goal is to help them grow to their market size without adding too much fat. During this phase, ducks may consume 5-6 pounds of feed per week. This feed will be slightly lower in protein than the grower feed, but still rich enough to support their weight gain.

It's important to feed the ducks enough to reach market weight in a reasonable time, but not too much that they become overweight or develop fatty meat. Keep checking their weight regularly and make sure they're growing at a healthy pace. You may need to adjust the amount of feed depending on how they're doing. If the ducks are gaining weight too quickly, reduce the feed slightly. On the other hand, if their weight gain is slow, you can increase the amount of feed.

Free-Choice vs. Scheduled Feeding

Some duck farmers prefer to feed their ducks on a scheduled basis, providing them with feed twice a day, while others allow free-choice feeding, where ducks can eat whenever they are hungry. With free-choice feeding, ducks have access to food at all times, and they eat as much as they want. While this method is convenient, it requires careful monitoring to avoid overfeeding. Free-choice feeding works best when you have a good system in place for managing feed and ensuring that the ducks do not gain excessive weight.

If you choose scheduled feeding, make sure you are providing enough food at each feeding to meet the ducks' nutritional needs. Twice a day feeding is common, but you can adjust the feeding times based on your ducks' growth patterns.

Avoiding Overfeeding and Maintaining Health

Regardless of whether you choose scheduled or free-choice feeding, always monitor the ducks' health closely. Overfeeding can lead to obesity, which may result in fatty meat, lower quality of the ducks' health, and increased risk of disease. Make sure to observe their body condition, and adjust the feed amount as needed.

Incorporating Foraging And Grazing For Natural Diet Supplementation

While most of the nutrition ducks need comes from commercial feed, allowing them to forage and graze outdoors can be a great way to supplement their diet. Ducks are natural foragers, and they enjoy eating grasses, weeds, insects, and even small amphibians. This natural behavior not only helps them get extra nutrition but also contributes to their overall health and the quality of their meat.

Benefits of Foraging and Grazing

Ducks have a strong instinct to forage for food, and when they are allowed to roam outdoors, they can gather a variety of food items from their environment. This natural diet includes a range of plant materials like grasses, weeds, and seeds, as well as insects, worms, and small animals. Foraging provides ducks with extra vitamins, minerals, and proteins that may not be present in their commercial feed.

When ducks are free to graze on quality pasture, they can meet a significant portion of their nutritional needs through foraging. Depending on the quality of the pasture and how much time the ducks spend outdoors, foraging can make up 50-70% of their diet. The nutrients they get from foraging can improve their overall health and help them develop stronger immune systems. Ducks that graze on good pasture may also have a healthier balance of fats in their bodies, which can lead to higher-quality meat with better taste and texture.

Foraging also helps keep ducks engaged and active, which is good for their mental and physical health. When ducks are allowed to explore and forage, they are less likely to experience stress or boredom, both of which can lead to health problems. Grazing and foraging can also reduce the need for additional feeding, which can lower feed costs, making this a more economical option for farmers.

Foraging as a Supplement, Not a Replacement

While foraging offers many benefits, it should not be relied upon as the sole source of nutrition for ducks. Commercial feed is specially designed to provide ducks with all the essential nutrients they need for proper growth, health, and meat production. Foraging, while beneficial, may not provide all of the necessary nutrients in the right amounts. For example, ducks may not get enough protein or certain vitamins from foraging alone, especially if the pasture is poor or not varied enough.

Therefore, foraging should be seen as a supplement to the main diet rather than a replacement. Ducks that forage will still need to be fed a balanced diet of commercial feed that is formulated to meet their nutritional needs. The feed should be high in protein, vitamins, minerals, and energy to ensure that the ducks grow properly and stay healthy.

Balancing Foraging with Commercial Feed

To get the best results, farmers should aim to balance foraging with the right amount of commercial feed. This means providing access to high-quality feed while allowing ducks to forage for a portion of their diet. The amount of feed you provide will depend on how much the ducks are able to forage and how much supplemental nutrition they need. For instance, if the ducks are grazing on a pasture with lots of insects and plants, they may need less feed than ducks that are kept in an area with less foraging opportunity.

Farmers should also monitor the health of their ducks closely. If you notice that the ducks are not gaining weight at the desired rate or showing signs of malnutrition, it may be a sign that they need more feed or a more balanced pasture. Regularly checking the ducks' overall condition will help ensure they are getting the right amount of nutrients for healthy growth.

Best Practices for Foraging

To make the most of foraging, it's important to provide ducks with access to a safe, clean, and varied environment. High-quality pasture with a range of plants and insects will give ducks the best nutrition. It's also important to rotate grazing areas to prevent overgrazing, which can damage the pasture and reduce the quality of the forage.

If you're raising ducks in a free-range system, make sure they have access to plenty of space to roam and forage. Ducks should be able to access fresh grass, weeds, and insects, which will enrich their diet and help improve the flavor of their meat.

Cost-Effective Feeding Strategies: Reducing Waste And Maximizing Efficiency

Feeding ducks can be expensive, and one of the biggest challenges farmers face is minimizing waste while ensuring their ducks get enough nutrition. Ducks can be wasteful eaters, especially if feed is scattered on the ground, leading to feed being lost or spoiled. However, there are several strategies you can use to reduce waste and make your feeding program more efficient, helping you save money in the long run.

1. Use Proper Feeders

One of the most effective ways to reduce feed waste is by using proper feeders. Ducks tend to waste feed when it is scattered on the ground or when they are able to spill it easily. To prevent this, invest in feeders that are designed to minimize waste.

Raised feeders or trough-style feeders are great options. Raised feeders help prevent ducks from throwing feed out of the trough by keeping it in a contained space. This also makes it easier for ducks to eat the feed without getting it dirty or scattered all over the ground. By ensuring the ducks have easy access to their feed in an organized manner, you can cut down on waste and make sure the feed is eaten rather than wasted.

2. Manage Feed Storage

Proper feed storage is crucial to reduce spoilage and waste. If feed is not stored correctly, it can become moldy or attract pests, making it unsafe or unusable for your ducks. To avoid this, make sure your feed is stored in a dry, cool place where it is protected from moisture and pests like rodents or insects.

Using airtight containers or sealed bins can keep feed fresh and prevent contamination. Always check your feed regularly to ensure that it's still good to use. If you find any signs of spoilage, such as mold or an off smell, dispose of it immediately. Storing your feed properly ensures that it lasts longer and prevents you from having to buy more feed than necessary.

3. Monitor Feeding Habits

It's important to keep an eye on how much feed your ducks are actually consuming. Overfeeding is a common problem, especially if you are unsure how much they need. Providing too much feed can lead to waste, as ducks may leave food behind or spill it.

On the other hand, underfeeding can cause growth problems or health issues for your ducks, so it's essential to find the right balance. The amount of feed will depend on the age, size, and growth rate of your ducks. For example, younger ducks may eat smaller amounts but more frequently, while older ducks may consume larger portions. Regularly monitor how much your ducks are eating and adjust the feed amount as needed. You can measure how much feed you give them and compare it to how much is left at the end of the day to get a sense of their consumption.

By adjusting the quantity of feed to match the ducks' needs, you can prevent waste while making sure they get enough nutrition for healthy growth.

4. Supplement with Forage

Another cost-effective strategy is to supplement your ducks' diet with foraged food. Ducks are natural foragers and will happily eat grasses, weeds, insects, and other available plant matter. By allowing your ducks to forage for a portion of their diet, you can reduce the amount of commercial feed they need, which can save you money.

If you raise your ducks in a free-range or pasture system, they will likely spend a lot of time grazing and foraging. This not only reduces your feed costs but also provides your ducks with a more natural and varied diet, which can improve their health and the quality of the meat they produce. However, it's important to remember that foraging should only supplement their diet and not replace it entirely. Ducks still need a balanced feed that provides all the necessary nutrients for healthy growth and development.

Make sure the area where your ducks are foraging is safe and provides nutritious food. You can also plant specific forage crops like clover, which are rich in protein and other nutrients beneficial to ducks. Regularly check the pasture to ensure that it is free of harmful plants or chemicals that could be harmful to your ducks.

5. Practice Good Feed Management

In addition to monitoring feeding amounts and supplementing with foraged food, practicing good feed management overall can help reduce waste. One simple but effective way to manage feed is to feed your ducks smaller portions throughout the day rather than giving them one large serving at once. This ensures that they eat the feed without it being left out for too long, reducing waste.

It's also helpful to clean feeders regularly. Dirty feeders can cause feed to become contaminated, leading to waste and potential health issues for your ducks. Clean feeders and waterers can encourage ducks to eat more efficiently, which can further reduce waste.

Chapter 5

HEALTH MANAGEMENT AND DISEASE PREVENTION

Common Health Issues And Diseases In Meat Ducks

Raising ducks for meat can be a rewarding experience, but just like any farm animals, ducks are vulnerable to certain health issues and diseases. Being able to spot problems early and taking action quickly is important for keeping your ducks healthy and ensuring good meat production. Here are some of the most common health issues that can affect ducks:

1. Respiratory Issues

Ducks are prone to respiratory problems, especially if they are kept in poorly ventilated spaces or if their living area is dirty. Ammonia, which is produced by their droppings, can build up and irritate their respiratory system. This makes them more susceptible to infections. Respiratory diseases such as avian influenza (bird flu) and duck plague (duck viral enteritis) can spread quickly and cause serious symptoms. If your ducks are suffering from respiratory problems, you might notice them having trouble breathing, coughing, or showing nasal discharge. Early treatment is important to prevent these diseases from spreading to other ducks.

2. Coccidiosis

Coccidiosis is a parasitic infection that affects the digestive system of ducks, particularly in young birds. This disease can cause symptoms such as diarrhea, lethargy (weakness or tiredness), and poor growth. In severe cases, coccidiosis can be fatal if not treated properly. It is important to maintain clean living conditions to reduce the risk of coccidiosis, as the parasite spreads through contaminated feed, water, and bedding. If you notice signs of illness like diarrhea and poor growth in your ducklings, it's crucial to seek veterinary advice and possibly treat them with medication to control the infection.

3. Foot and Leg Problems

Ducks are prone to foot and leg issues, particularly if they are kept in wet or dirty environments. Conditions like bumblefoot, a bacterial infection in the feet, can be painful and cause swelling, which may make it hard for ducks to walk or move freely. If left untreated, it can cause permanent damage and affect their ability to forage or grow properly. Other common leg problems include lameness, which can occur if ducks injure themselves or develop infections. It's important to keep their living area dry and clean to help prevent foot and leg problems. Regularly inspect your ducks' legs and feet to catch any signs of injury or infection early.

4. Parasites

Parasites, both external and internal, can cause a range of health issues in ducks. External parasites like lice, mites, and fleas can irritate the skin, leading to itching and discomfort. These parasites can also affect the ducks' feather quality, causing them to lose feathers and suffer from poor plumage. Internal parasites, such as worms, can also be a problem, causing symptoms like weight loss, poor growth, and digestive issues. To control parasites, it's important to keep your ducks' living area clean and to regularly check them for signs of external parasites. If you suspect internal parasites, a vet can recommend deworming treatment to help keep your ducks healthy.

5. Fungal Infections

Fungal infections are another potential health issue for ducks, especially in environments that are damp and wet. Aspergillosis is one such fungal infection that affects the respiratory system. Ducks infected with aspergillosis may show signs like coughing, wheezing, or difficulty breathing. Wet bedding or poor ventilation in their housing can contribute to fungal growth, which increases the risk of infection. To prevent fungal infections, it's essential to maintain clean, dry living conditions and ensure proper airflow in their housing. If your ducks show signs of respiratory distress, it's important to seek veterinary treatment to manage the infection before it spreads.

Preventative Measures

Being aware of these common health issues is just the first step in keeping your ducks healthy. There are a few preventative measures that can help reduce the risk of disease and improve the overall health of your ducks:

• Good hygiene: Keep the ducks' living area clean, dry, and well-ventilated. Clean bedding regularly to avoid the build-up of harmful bacteria and parasites.

• Proper nutrition: Provide a balanced diet to support strong immune systems. Nutritional deficiencies can make ducks more vulnerable to illness.

• Monitor health regularly: Keep a close eye on your ducks for any signs of illness, such as changes in behavior, eating habits, or physical appearance. The sooner you spot a problem, the sooner you can address it.

• Quarantine new birds: If you bring in new ducks or hatchlings, it's a good idea to isolate them from your main flock for a few weeks to ensure they are not carrying any diseases.

• Veterinary care: If you notice any symptoms of illness or suspect your ducks might have a disease, consult a veterinarian immediately for proper diagnosis and treatment.

Signs Of Illness: Early Detection And Prevention Techniques

Detecting illness early in your ducks is important for preventing more serious health issues. Many health problems in ducks start with small, subtle changes in behavior or appearance, so regular observation is key to identifying problems before they worsen. The sooner you can spot signs of illness, the quicker you can take action to treat your ducks and prevent the disease from spreading to other birds. Here are some common signs to look out for and tips on how to detect illness early:

Common Signs of Illness in Ducks

1. Lethargy

One of the first signs that a duck may be sick is a change in its activity level. Healthy ducks are usually active, moving around, foraging, and interacting with other ducks. If you notice that a duck is staying in one place more than usual, not moving much, or resting when it would normally be active, it could be a sign of illness. Lethargy often indicates that a duck is not feeling well and may need to be examined for other symptoms.

2. Changes in Appetite

Ducks that suddenly stop eating or drinking may be sick. A healthy duck should have a strong appetite, and it should be drinking plenty of water. If you notice a duck refusing food or water, or drinking excessively, it may indicate digestive issues, infections, or other health problems. Changes in appetite should never be ignored, as they can be a sign of a serious illness.

3. Abnormal Droppings

The appearance of duck droppings can tell you a lot about their health. Healthy duck droppings are typically firm, brown, and may have a white, urate portion. If the droppings become watery, dark, or unusual in color, it could be a sign of digestive problems, infections, or parasites. Diarrhea, in particular, is often a sign of coccidiosis, a common parasitic infection in young ducks. Keep an eye on the consistency and color of your ducks' droppings and take note of any changes.

4. Respiratory Symptoms

Respiratory problems in ducks are common and can be a sign of infection. If you hear sneezing, coughing, or wheezing, or notice nasal discharge or labored breathing, this may indicate a respiratory infection. Infections like avian influenza or duck plague can spread quickly, so it's important to monitor these symptoms closely. If you observe any of these signs, it's essential to separate the sick duck from the rest of the flock and consult a veterinarian for proper treatment.

5. Changes in Feathers or Skin

The condition of a duck's feathers and skin can give you clues about its health. Healthy ducks have shiny, smooth feathers, and their skin is typically clean. If you notice feather loss, dull or ragged feathers, or skin lesions, it could be a sign of parasites, fungal infections, or other skin problems. Parasites like lice, mites, and fleas can cause itching and irritation, leading to feather damage. It's important to check your ducks regularly for any signs of external parasites or skin conditions.

6. Swelling

Swelling around the face, neck, or legs of a duck can signal an infection or injury. Swelling could be the result of an abscess, a bacterial infection, or even a serious illness like fowl cholera or duck viral enteritis. If you notice any unusual swelling, it's important to act quickly, as it can indicate a serious condition that may require medical attention.

Early Detection and Prevention Tips

To detect illness early and prevent the spread of disease, it's important to regularly observe your ducks and keep track of their behavior, appetite, and overall condition. Here are some tips to help you detect and prevent illness:

1. Regular Observation

Make it a habit to check your ducks every day. Look for any changes in behavior, such as lethargy, changes in eating habits, or abnormal droppings. Take note of their physical appearance—are their feathers looking dull, or is there any swelling? Early detection is key, so make sure you spend time observing your ducks each day.

2. Isolate Sick Ducks

If you notice any ducks showing signs of illness, it's a good idea to isolate them from the rest of the flock to prevent the spread of disease. Keeping sick ducks away from healthy ones helps reduce the risk of infections spreading. Make sure the sick duck has access to fresh water and food, and consult a veterinarian to determine the cause of the illness.

3. Maintain Good Hygiene

Good farm hygiene is one of the best ways to prevent illness in ducks. Clean their living area regularly, replace wet bedding, and ensure their drinking water is fresh and clean. A clean environment reduces the risk of bacterial, viral, and parasitic infections. It's also important to remove any waste or spoiled food that might attract pests or cause contamination.

4. Quarantine New Ducks

If you bring in new ducks to your farm, it's important to quarantine them for a few weeks before introducing them to your main flock. This helps prevent the spread of any diseases or infections that they may carry. Keep the new ducks in a separate area and monitor them for signs of illness before allowing them to mingle with your other ducks.

5. Consult a Veterinarian

If you observe any signs of illness in your ducks, it's important to consult a veterinarian as soon as possible. Early diagnosis and treatment are crucial for preventing the spread of disease and ensuring the health of your flock. A veterinarian can help you identify the cause of illness and recommend appropriate treatment.

Vaccination And Parasite Management For Meat Ducks

Vaccination and parasite management are crucial parts of keeping your ducks healthy and ensuring good meat quality. Vaccines protect your ducks from harmful diseases, while managing parasites helps prevent weight loss, stress, and other health problems. Here's a simple guide to both practices:

Vaccination for Ducks

Vaccines are an important way to prevent common diseases that could harm your ducks or spread quickly within your flock. While not all diseases have vaccines, there are several key vaccines that you should consider for your ducks to keep them healthy and safe.

1. Duck Viral Enteritis (Duck Plague)

Duck Viral Enteritis, also known as duck plague, is a highly contagious and often fatal disease in ducks. It affects their immune system and can spread rapidly among your flock. Symptoms include sudden death, diarrhea, and nasal discharge. The good news is that there is a vaccine available for this disease, and vaccinating your ducks early can provide strong protection against it. This vaccine is especially important if you are raising ducks in large numbers or in areas where the disease is common.

2. Avian Influenza

Avian Influenza (bird flu) is a viral disease that can spread quickly through a poultry flock, causing serious illness or death. It is a major concern for all types of poultry, including ducks. While the disease can sometimes be controlled through good biosecurity practices, vaccination offers an added layer of protection, especially in areas where outbreaks are more frequent. Vaccinating your ducks can help reduce the risk of an outbreak in your flock and prevent losses.

3. Newcastle Disease

Newcastle Disease is another viral infection that affects poultry, including ducks. It can cause respiratory problems, digestive issues, and even death in severe cases. It is highly contagious and can spread rapidly within a flock. The good news is that there is a vaccine available for Newcastle Disease. Vaccinating your ducks can help protect them from this disease, especially if you live in an area where it is known to occur frequently. This vaccine is recommended to prevent outbreaks and maintain the health of your flock.

Parasite Management for Ducks

Parasites, both internal and external, can significantly affect the health of your ducks, leading to poor growth, weight loss, and lower meat quality. Managing parasites is just as important as vaccination in ensuring the overall well-being of your ducks.

1. Internal Parasites

Internal parasites, such as worms, are common in ducks and can cause digestive problems, weight loss, and poor growth. They can also make your ducks more susceptible to other diseases. Regular deworming treatments can help control these internal parasites and keep your ducks healthy. Deworming products are available in various forms, including oral medications and injections, and should be used according to the instructions from your veterinarian.

It is important to monitor your ducks for signs of internal parasites, which may include weight loss, diarrhea, and poor feather condition. If you notice these symptoms, it's a good idea to consult a veterinarian to confirm the presence of worms and to get a recommended treatment plan.

2. External Parasites

External parasites like mites, lice, and fleas are another concern for duck health. These parasites can cause skin irritation, stress, and discomfort for your ducks. In addition to affecting their health, external parasites can also impact the quality of the meat, as stressed ducks do not grow as efficiently.

To manage external parasites, you should regularly check your ducks for signs of infestation, such as excessive scratching, feather loss, or visible pests on their skin. If you find signs of an infestation, consult a veterinarian for safe and effective treatments. There are several approved products available, such as sprays or powders, that can help eliminate these external parasites.

In addition to using treatments, it's important to maintain clean living conditions for your ducks. Clean their housing regularly and remove any wet bedding or manure, as this creates an environment where parasites thrive. Keeping their living area dry and clean is an effective way to reduce the risk of infestations.

Developing a Parasite Management Plan

The best way to manage parasites on your farm is by working with a veterinarian to develop a parasite management plan tailored to your specific needs. A vet can guide you on the most appropriate deworming schedule, the best treatments for external parasites, and how to monitor your flock for any signs of illness or infestation. Regular check-ups with your vet will also help ensure that any issues are caught early and treated promptly.

Biosecurity Practices To Prevent Disease Spread

Biosecurity is a set of practices that help prevent diseases from spreading on your farm. Keeping your ducks healthy and safe from illness is essential for a successful meat duck operation. By following good biosecurity practices, you can reduce the risk of diseases entering your flock and affecting their health. Here are some key biosecurity measures you can follow to protect your ducks:

1. Isolate New Ducks

When you bring in new ducks or ducklings, it's important to keep them separate from the rest of your flock for at least 30 days. This isolation period, also called quarantine, helps prevent the spread of any diseases that the new ducks might carry. Sometimes, ducks can have infections that don't show symptoms right away, so isolating them gives you time to observe and make sure they are healthy before they interact with the rest of your flock. Quarantining new arrivals is a simple but effective way to protect your entire flock from possible infections.

2. Control Access to the Farm

Limiting visitors to your farm and controlling who enters your duck area is another important biosecurity measure. People can carry germs on their shoes, clothing, or equipment, and these germs can easily spread to your ducks. To prevent this, make sure that anyone who comes onto your farm follows strict hygiene practices. This includes washing their hands, disinfecting their boots or shoes, and changing into clean clothing before entering the duck area. By controlling who enters and ensuring that visitors take proper hygiene measures, you can greatly reduce the risk of introducing diseases to your ducks.

3. Clean and Disinfect Regularly

Keeping your duck housing, feeding areas, and equipment clean is a critical part of biosecurity. Regular cleaning and disinfecting help remove harmful bacteria, viruses, and pathogens that could cause illness. This is especially important after any outbreaks of disease or when introducing new ducks. Be sure to clean all surfaces, including the floors, walls, feeders, and waterers, to reduce the buildup of harmful microorganisms. Use disinfectants that are safe for animals and effective against common poultry diseases. Establish a regular cleaning schedule and stick to it to ensure that your farm remains hygienic and disease-free.

4. Monitor Wild Birds

Wild birds can be a major source of disease for domestic ducks. They can carry diseases like avian influenza, which can spread quickly to your flock. To protect your ducks, it's important to prevent wild birds from coming into contact with them. You can do this by using netting or fencing around your pens to keep wild birds out. Avoid feeding wild birds near your farm, as this can attract them to your ducks. Additionally, avoid having open water sources that wild birds might use, as they can carry diseases in their droppings or feathers. By keeping wild birds away from your ducks, you reduce the risk of disease transmission from outside sources.

5. Provide Proper Ventilation

Proper ventilation is essential for maintaining a healthy environment for your ducks. Poor ventilation can lead to high humidity and damp conditions, which are ideal for the growth of harmful bacteria and fungi. These conditions can contribute to respiratory diseases in your ducks. To prevent this, make sure that your duck housing is well-ventilated. Good airflow will help keep the air fresh, dry, and clean, reducing the risk of respiratory infections. Additionally, proper ventilation helps remove ammonia fumes from duck waste, which can irritate the ducks' eyes and respiratory systems. Keeping the housing dry is also important to prevent fungal growth, which can lead to diseases like aspergillosis.

6. Disinfect Transport Vehicles and Equipment

If you transport ducks or any equipment off the farm, always clean and disinfect the vehicles and equipment when they return. Vehicles used for transporting ducks can carry disease-causing pathogens that might spread to your farm. Clean the interior of the vehicles, including cages or crates, and disinfect any equipment before it's used with your ducks. This ensures that nothing brought in from outside can infect your flock.

7. Establish a Disease Surveillance System

A good way to keep track of the health of your flock is to establish a disease surveillance system. Regularly check for signs of illness in your ducks and record any health issues you notice. This allows you to catch potential outbreaks early before they spread to other ducks. If you notice anything unusual, isolate the affected ducks and consult a veterinarian for advice. Keeping records of the health of your ducks and their living conditions can help you identify patterns and prevent future disease outbreaks.

Managing Stress And Its Impact On Duck Health And Meat Quality

Stress is a major factor that can negatively affect both the health of ducks and the quality of their meat. Ducks that are stressed are more likely to become sick, have weaker immune systems, and grow slower. Additionally, stress can lower the quality of the meat, making it less tender, less flavorful, and resulting in smaller yields. To raise healthy ducks and produce high-quality meat, it is crucial to minimize stress as much as possible.

Common Stressors for Ducks

Ducks, like other animals, can become stressed for various reasons. Identifying and addressing the causes of stress is important for the well-being of the ducks and the quality of the meat they produce. Some of the most common stressors for ducks include:

1. Poor Housing Conditions:

Overcrowding, dirty living environments, and lack of space are significant stressors for ducks. When ducks are crowded together, they cannot move freely, which increases stress and makes them more vulnerable to diseases. Dirty bedding, wet conditions, or poorly maintained living spaces can also cause stress by creating an uncomfortable or unhygienic environment for the ducks. Ducks need enough room to move around comfortably and clean bedding to rest on. Keeping their living area clean and spacious is essential for their well-being.

2. Sudden Changes in Environment:

Ducks are sensitive to changes in their surroundings. Sudden shifts in temperature, light, or diet can be stressful for them. For example, abrupt temperature changes or exposure to extreme weather conditions can cause physical stress and discomfort. Likewise, if the lighting is changed too suddenly (for example, moving from dark to bright light), it can disturb the ducks. Introducing new types of food or changing their feeding schedule can also cause stress, as it disrupts their regular routine. Gradually introducing changes and ensuring a stable environment helps reduce stress.

3. Handling:

Rough handling or excessive human interaction can cause stress in ducks. Ducks are naturally wary of humans, and being handled too much or in a rough manner can be upsetting to them. If ducks feel threatened or scared by human presence, it can lead to increased stress levels, which affects their overall health. It's important to handle ducks gently and avoid unnecessary contact. Keeping human interaction to a minimum can help ducks feel safer and more at ease.

4. Inadequate Food and Water:

Lack of access to sufficient food and clean water is another major stressor for ducks. Ducks need a consistent supply of nutritious food and fresh water to grow properly and stay healthy. If they are not provided with enough food or water, they will become stressed and their growth will suffer. Stress from hunger or dehydration can lead to poor health and weaker immune systems, making them more susceptible to diseases. Ensure that your ducks always have access to clean water and food in adequate amounts to keep them healthy and stress-free.

How to Reduce Stress and Improve Duck Health

To reduce stress and promote better health and meat quality, there are several strategies you can use to create a calm and comfortable environment for your ducks:

1. Provide Adequate Space:

Make sure your ducks have enough space to move freely. Overcrowding can lead to stress, so avoid keeping too many ducks in one area. Give each duck enough room to move, rest, and eat comfortably. The more space they have, the less stress they will experience.

2. Maintain a Clean and Comfortable Environment:

Keep your ducks' living area clean and dry. Regularly change bedding, remove waste, and make sure their housing is well-ventilated. Dirty or wet conditions can lead to stress and health problems. Cleanliness also helps prevent the spread of disease, which can cause additional stress.

3. Control Temperature and Lighting:

Ducks should be kept in an environment with stable temperature and lighting conditions. Avoid extreme temperature fluctuations, and ensure they are not exposed to extreme heat or cold. Gradually adjust lighting to avoid shocking the ducks, especially when moving them to new areas. Consistent lighting and temperature will help keep your ducks comfortable.

4. Minimize Handling and Disruptions:

Try to minimize how often and how roughly you handle your ducks. Avoid unnecessary handling or excessive human contact, as this can increase stress. Ducks prefer to feel safe and undisturbed, so try to let them go about their activities without interruption. If you need to handle them, do so gently and calmly to avoid startling them.

5. Ensure Constant Access to Fresh Food and Water:

Always make sure that your ducks have access to plenty of clean water and nutritious food. This helps prevent stress from hunger or dehydration, which can negatively affect their growth and health. Regularly check that the food and water are fresh and readily available.

The Benefits of Reducing Stress

By reducing stress in your ducks, you can improve their overall health, growth, and meat quality. Ducks that are less stressed will have a stronger immune system, grow at a healthy rate, and produce meat that is tender, flavorful, and of higher quality. Healthy, stress-free ducks are also less likely to suffer from diseases, which can further enhance the productivity and profitability of your farm.

Chapter 6

GROWTH STAGES AND MANAGING DUCKS FROM DUCKLING TO MARKET WEIGHT

Brooding Young Ducklings: Setting Up A Brooding Area

The first few weeks of a duckling's life are very important for its growth and health. During this time, it is essential to provide a comfortable, safe, and warm environment for them to thrive. Ducklings are particularly sensitive to temperature, so getting the brooding area right is key to preventing health problems and ensuring they grow strong.

Creating the Right Brooding Area

A brooding area is a space where ducklings are kept during their early weeks. This area should be both spacious and cozy enough to provide the warmth they need. Ducklings need a place where they can move around but also have a warm spot to stay when needed.

For the first week of life, the temperature in the brooding area should be around 90°F (32°C). Ducklings cannot regulate their body temperature well at this stage, so warmth is very important. After the first week, you can gradually lower the temperature by about 5°F each week until it reaches about 70°F (21°C), by the time they are around 4-6 weeks old. This gradual change helps the ducklings adjust to cooler temperatures as they grow and become more independent.

Heating and Temperature Control

To keep the brooding area warm, use heat lamps or brooders. Heat lamps are a good way to provide direct warmth, but make sure they are set up in a way that allows the ducklings to move away from the heat if they get too warm. Ducklings will naturally move to the cooler areas of the brooding space if they need to, so it's important to make sure they have enough room to find a comfortable temperature. Never let the area get too hot, as it can lead to overheating, which can stress the ducklings and cause health problems.

Bedding for Comfort and Cleanliness

Ducklings need clean, dry bedding to stay healthy. Use absorbent bedding material such as straw, wood shavings, or rice hulls. These materials help soak up any moisture and keep the area dry, which is essential for the health of the ducklings. Wet bedding can lead to problems such as foot infections and other health issues, so it's important to change the bedding regularly.

Check the bedding daily to make sure it's clean and dry, and replace it as needed. Keeping the brooding area dry will also help reduce the risk of disease and ensure the ducklings are comfortable.

Feeding and Watering the Ducklings

Ducklings need easy access to food and water to grow healthy and strong. Make sure the food and water containers are placed within easy reach, so the ducklings can easily access them. Ducklings often dip their bills into the water to help with digestion, so always ensure that they have fresh, clean water available at all times.

For food, provide a high-protein starter feed that contains around 18-20% protein. This type of feed is specially formulated to support the rapid growth of ducklings in the first few weeks. Ducklings grow quickly during this period, and they need plenty of protein to develop strong muscles and bones. You can feed them several times a day, offering enough food so that they can eat as much as they want.

General Care Tips for Ducklings

It's important to keep a close eye on the ducklings in the brooding area. Make sure they are eating, drinking, and staying warm enough. If the ducklings are huddling together under the heat lamp, it may mean they are too cold, and you should increase the temperature. On the other hand, if they are scattered away from the heat, it may be too hot, and you should decrease the temperature.

If you notice any ducklings acting weak, not eating or drinking, or showing signs of illness, it's important to address the issue right away. Healthy, active ducklings are a sign that your brooding setup is working well.

Caring For Ducklings: Feeding, Temperature Control, And Cleanliness

Taking care of ducklings properly in their first few weeks is essential to make sure they grow strong and healthy. Ducklings are very sensitive to their environment, so it's important to provide the right conditions to help them develop well. This includes giving them the right food, controlling the temperature in their brooding area, and keeping the space clean.

Feeding Ducklings

During the first few weeks, ducklings need a high-protein starter feed that is specifically made for them. This feed should have about 18-20% protein, which is important for their rapid growth. Protein helps build strong muscles and bones. In addition to protein, the starter feed should contain vitamins, minerals, and fats, all of which support their overall health and development.

Ducklings grow very quickly during their first few weeks, so they need a lot of energy to keep up with their fast development. You should make sure that they always have access to food. As the ducklings grow older, you can start adding small amounts of natural foods like grains, chopped greens, or even insects to their diet. However, their main source of nutrition should still come from the starter feed. This will make sure they get all the essential nutrients they need to grow strong and healthy.

Controlling the Temperature

Temperature control is one of the most important factors in caring for ducklings. They are very sensitive to temperature changes, especially in their first few weeks. If they are too cold, ducklings can become sluggish, weak, and may even become ill. On the other hand, if they are too hot, they may become stressed, dehydrated, or have trouble breathing.

The ideal temperature for ducklings in the first week is about 90°F (32°C). You can gradually reduce the temperature by 5°F (about 3°C) each week until it reaches around 70°F (21°C) by the time they are 4 to 6 weeks old. You can use a heat lamp or a brooder to provide warmth. However, it's important to monitor the ducklings carefully to make sure they are comfortable.

To tell if the ducklings are the right temperature, watch their behavior. If they are crowding under the heat source, they may be too cold, and you should increase the temperature. If they are moving away from the heat, they might be too hot, and you should lower the temperature. The key is to adjust the heat source so that the ducklings have the option to move closer to or farther from it depending on their needs.

Keeping the Brooding Area Clean

Ducklings are messy eaters and drinkers, so keeping their living area clean is very important. They can quickly dirty their bedding, food, and water, which can lead to infections or other health issues if not cleaned regularly. A clean environment helps prevent the spread of disease and keeps the ducklings healthy.

You should clean the ducklings' bedding, waterers, and food containers every day. Replace soiled bedding with fresh, dry bedding to avoid the buildup of bacteria or mold. Wet or dirty bedding can lead to foot infections or other problems, so it's crucial to keep the area dry and clean. Ensure that the ducklings always have access to clean water, as they need it not only for drinking but also for dipping their bills to help with digestion.

In addition to cleaning the area, regularly check that the food and water containers are not contaminated with droppings or bedding. This will help keep the ducklings' environment sanitary and reduce the risk of infections. Always make sure that the food is fresh and that the water is clean, as dirty water or stale food can cause health problems for the ducklings.

Other Care Tips

In addition to feeding, temperature control, and cleanliness, there are a few other things you should keep in mind when caring for ducklings:

- Observe their behavior: Always keep an eye on the ducklings and make sure they are eating, drinking, and behaving normally. If a duckling appears weak or is not eating, it may be sick and need attention.
- Avoid overcrowding: Make sure there is enough space for the ducklings to move around freely. Overcrowding can lead to stress, aggression, or injuries, and can make it harder to keep the area clean.
- Minimize stress: Ducklings can become stressed from too much handling, noise, or sudden changes in their environment. Try to keep their space quiet and calm to avoid stressing them out.

Juvenile Phase: Managing Space And Feeding For Optimal Growth

As ducklings grow, they enter the juvenile phase, which typically occurs between 4 and 8 weeks of age. During this stage, their nutritional and space needs change. They are no longer growing as rapidly as they did as ducklings, and their bodies are transitioning to a more steady weight gain. It's important to adjust their care to meet their new needs to ensure they continue to grow and stay healthy.

Space Requirements

As juvenile ducks become more active, they need more space to move around. If ducks are overcrowded, they can become stressed and may start acting aggressively toward one another. This can lead to injuries and make them more vulnerable to diseases. To avoid overcrowding, make sure each duck has enough room. If the ducks are kept indoors, provide at least 2-3 square feet of space per duck. This will allow them to move around freely, stretch their wings, and interact with each other.

If your ducks are free-ranging or living on pasture, they will need even more space to roam and forage. Ducks enjoy exploring and will benefit from having room to move and search for food. Giving them access to a large, clean, and dry area will promote their health and well-being. It is also essential to keep the area safe from predators by providing secure fencing or shelter.

Feeding Juvenile Ducks

At this stage, the feeding requirements of juvenile ducks change. They are still growing, but their growth is not as rapid as it was during the duckling stage. This means their feed should be adjusted to support more steady weight gain and development.

The protein content of their feed can be reduced to around 16-18%. While they still need plenty of nutrients to support healthy growth, they do not require the high-protein feed that they needed as ducklings. The reduced protein content helps prevent excessive fat buildup and encourages a more balanced, steady growth rate.

At this stage, you can begin to introduce grains into their diet. Corn, oats, and barley are good options. These grains can be mixed with their formulated feed to provide variety and additional energy. However, keep in mind that formulated feed should still make up the majority of their diet. This will ensure that they continue to receive all the essential vitamins, minerals, and nutrients that they need to grow strong and healthy.

In addition to the grains, you can also start offering natural forage, such as grasses, weeds, and insects. Ducks love foraging, and this provides them with a variety of nutrients that can supplement their diet. Natural forage also helps reduce feed costs, as the ducks will eat what they find in their environment. Just be sure that the forage is safe and free from pesticides or harmful plants.

Make sure that fresh, clean water is always available. Ducks drink a lot of water, and it's important for their digestion and overall health. They often dip their bills into the water to help with eating and digesting their food, so clean water is essential for their well-being.

Exercise and Activity

Juvenile ducks are full of energy and need plenty of opportunities to move around and exercise. Physical activity helps them develop strong muscles, maintain a healthy weight, and avoid obesity. If your ducks are not free-ranging, ensure that they have access to a larger pen or outdoor area where they can move around freely. A larger space allows them to exercise, stretch their legs, and interact with each other.

Healthy movement also helps prevent stress and aggression, which can occur in ducks that are kept in small, confined spaces. By giving them enough room to exercise, you will ensure that your ducks grow with a strong, well-balanced body. Ducks that don't get enough exercise may become overweight, which can lead to health issues and slower growth. Encouraging exercise through a spacious environment will keep your ducks happy and healthy.

Maintaining a Healthy Environment

In addition to feeding and space, maintaining a clean and dry living environment is important for juvenile ducks. Make sure their pen or housing is kept clean and dry to prevent the buildup of bacteria or harmful parasites. Ducks can be messy, so regularly clean their bedding and replace it as needed to keep their space comfortable.

It's also important to protect juvenile ducks from extreme weather conditions. Ensure that they have shelter from the rain and cold, and provide shaded areas if it gets too hot. Temperature control is still important at this stage, so make sure they are not exposed to extreme temperatures that could harm their health.

Preparing Ducks For Market: Diet Adjustments And Growth Monitoring

As ducks near the end of their growth period, typically around 8 weeks, it's important to make specific adjustments to their diet and care to ensure they reach the optimal size for market. This final stage focuses on steady growth and muscle development, while preventing excessive fat accumulation. Proper preparation during this phase helps produce high-quality meat and ensures that the ducks are ready for slaughter at the right time.

Diet Adjustments

In the last few weeks before slaughter, you'll want to adjust the ducks' diet to support the final stages of their growth. One key change is reducing the protein content of their feed to about 14-16%. At this point, ducks no longer need as much protein because they are moving from rapid growth to muscle development. Lowering the protein level helps minimize fat deposition, which can improve the quality of the meat.

Instead of the high-protein feed used earlier, provide ducks with a balanced finisher diet. This type of feed is designed to support healthy growth during the final phase. A good finisher feed includes a mix of grains, fats, and vitamins, ensuring that the ducks get the necessary nutrients for muscle growth and overall health. Grains like corn, oats, and barley are common in finisher diets and provide the energy ducks need for their final growth spurt.

In addition to feed, access to clean, fresh water is essential. Ducks drink a lot of water, and proper hydration is crucial for muscle development, digestion, and maintaining a healthy body. Always make sure there is fresh water available, as it helps with overall growth and well-being.

Growth Monitoring

During this final phase, it's important to monitor the ducks' growth to ensure they are on track to reach market weight without becoming overweight or underweight. Regularly weigh your ducks to keep track of their progress. Weighing helps you determine whether the ducks are gaining weight at a steady pace and whether they are close to reaching the desired weight for market.

It's also important to monitor their body condition. Look for signs of healthy weight gain—ducks should appear well-rounded, but not excessively fat. Ducks that grow too fast may end up with poor meat quality, with excess fat and reduced muscle development. On the other hand, ducks that grow too slowly may not reach market weight on time, which could result in a delay or financial loss. Keeping a close eye on both weight and body condition will help you determine if the ducks are growing at the right pace.

Watch for any signs of stress or illness that might slow growth or impact meat quality. Ducks that are stressed or sick will not grow properly and may have lower-quality meat. Make sure the ducks are in a comfortable, clean, and safe environment to support healthy growth.

Environment and Care

In addition to monitoring diet and weight, providing the right environment for the ducks is crucial during this phase. Ensure that the ducks still have plenty of space to move around, as this helps prevent stress and supports healthy muscle development. Overcrowding can lead to aggression and poor growth, so it's important to maintain appropriate space for each duck.

Make sure the ducks are protected from harsh weather conditions. Ducks that are too hot or too cold can become stressed, which affects their growth. If you are raising ducks indoors, ensure that the space is well-ventilated and temperature-controlled. Outdoor ducks need access to shelter in case of extreme weather conditions.

It's also important to keep the living area clean and dry. Dirty conditions can lead to disease and parasites, which will harm the ducks and interfere with their growth. Regularly clean the pens, change the bedding, and remove any waste to maintain a healthy environment for the ducks.

Final Steps Before Market

As market day approaches, you should also consider the ducks' health and appearance. Healthy ducks with smooth feathers, good muscle development, and an appropriate body size are more likely to meet market standards. Make sure that the ducks have received proper care throughout their growth, and check them for any injuries or health issues that need attention.

On the day before slaughter, it's a good idea to limit feed to give the ducks time to empty their digestive systems. However, make sure they still have access to water so they remain hydrated. The right final preparations will help ensure that the ducks are in the best possible condition when they are processed.

Timing The Slaughter: Ideal Weight, Age, And Maturity

The timing of slaughter is very important when raising ducks for meat. If ducks are slaughtered too early, they may not have reached the right size or development, resulting in smaller, underdeveloped birds. On the other hand, waiting too long can lead to fatty or tough meat. The key to getting the best meat is to carefully monitor their weight, age, and overall maturity.

Ideal Weight

The ideal weight for meat ducks varies depending on the breed, but most commercial meat duck breeds like Pekin or Aylesbury should weigh between 6 and 8 pounds when they are ready for slaughter. Typically, ducks will reach this weight when they are around 8 to 10 weeks old. This is the general market age for many meat ducks, though some breeds may grow slightly faster or slower.

It's important to regularly check the weight of your ducks to make sure they are on track to reach the desired market weight. Weighing the ducks once a week can help you see how they are progressing. If they are not gaining weight at the expected rate, you may need to adjust their diet or make changes to their environment to help them grow.

Regular weight checks also help you avoid waiting too long to slaughter. Ducks that exceed the ideal weight range can start to accumulate too much fat, which can negatively affect the meat quality, making it less tender or flavorful. By monitoring their weight and adjusting their care as needed, you can ensure that the ducks are harvested at their best size.

Age and Maturity

Ducks typically reach market maturity between 8 and 10 weeks of age. At this stage, they should have developed a well-rounded body that shows a good balance of muscle and fat. This is the ideal time to slaughter, as the ducks are fully mature but not yet overgrown or fatty.

If ducks are slaughtered too early, they may not have enough muscle development, leading to less meat and potentially a less flavorful product. On the other hand, if ducks are kept for too long, they may have excessive fat, which can make the meat greasy or tough. Over-mature ducks may also have a firmer texture, which is less desirable for many consumers. For the best quality meat, the ducks should be slaughtered when they have reached their full size but not gone past the point of ideal maturity.

Maturity is more than just age—it's about how the ducks have developed in terms of muscle, fat, and overall health. Healthy ducks that are given the right care throughout their growth period will naturally reach maturity at the right time. Observing your ducks closely will help you know when they are ready. Signs of maturity include a full, rounded body and a healthy balance of muscle and fat. Their feathers should be thick and smooth, and they should be active and alert.

Monitoring Growth and Development

CHAPTER 6

To ensure the ducks are ready for slaughter at the right time, it's important to observe their growth regularly. Keep track of their weight and physical appearance, and pay attention to their behavior. Ducks that are not eating well or are acting lethargic may not be growing at the right rate and may need more attention. Ducks that are too active or too fat might be approaching the point where they have reached full maturity, so monitoring their condition is essential.

It's also important to consider how the ducks have been raised. Ducks that have had access to proper nutrition, exercise, and a clean, safe environment will grow at a healthy rate and will likely reach the ideal weight and maturity at the right time. Be sure to adjust their diet as they approach market age, making sure they are fed a balanced diet that promotes muscle development and prevents excess fat accumulation.

7

Chapter 7

PROCESSING AND BUTCHERING TECHNIQUES

Pre-Processing Preparations: Fasting And Transporting Ducks

Preparing ducks properly before processing is essential to ensure they are in the best condition for slaughter. Two important steps in this process are fasting and transportation. These steps help improve meat quality and make the processing smoother and more efficient.

Fasting Ducks Before Slaughter

Fasting ducks for a period of time before slaughter is a common practice in poultry processing. Typically, ducks are fasted for about 12 to 24 hours before they are slaughtered. The reason for fasting is to allow the ducks' digestive systems to empty out. This makes the processing and evisceration (removal of internal organs) much cleaner and easier. When the ducks' stomachs and intestines are empty, there is less waste that could get in the way or cause contamination during the processing. It also helps avoid any leftover undigested feed or debris that might spoil the meat, which can improve the overall quality of the product.

While the ducks should not be fed during this fasting period, it is essential that they still have access to clean, fresh water. Keeping the ducks hydrated is very important to prevent them from becoming dehydrated, which can lead to stress and lower meat quality. Providing water will also help ensure that their organs stay healthy and that they are not overly stressed by the fasting process.

It is important to note that fasting should not last too long, as extended periods without food or water can stress the ducks and negatively impact their health. A fasting period of 12 to 24 hours is generally sufficient to empty the digestive tract, while still keeping the ducks in a healthy, hydrated state.

Transporting Ducks to Processing

Once the ducks are ready for slaughter, they may need to be transported to a processing facility or another location for processing. This step must be handled with care to reduce stress and ensure that the ducks arrive in good condition.

Ducks are sensitive animals, and stressful transport conditions can negatively impact their health and the quality of the meat. Stress can cause a variety of problems, including increased heart rate, muscle tightening, and poor meat quality. Therefore, it is essential to keep the transport process as calm and stress-free as possible.

When transporting ducks, use well-ventilated containers or crates that allow the ducks to breathe comfortably. These containers should be spacious enough for the ducks to move around slightly but not so large that they are tossed around during the journey. Overcrowding should be avoided, as it can lead to stress, injury, or even suffocation.

The transport time should also be kept as short as possible. Prolonged journeys can increase stress levels in ducks, so planning a route that minimizes travel time is important. Ideally, the transportation process should be quick and direct to reduce the time the ducks are in transit.

Additionally, it is essential to control the temperature during transportation. Ducks are sensitive to extreme temperatures, so avoid exposing them to hot or cold weather during transport. In hot conditions, overheating can cause dehydration and stress, while cold temperatures can lead to hypothermia and illness. Ensure that the transportation area is well-ventilated and that the temperature remains within a comfortable range for the ducks.

It's also important to protect the ducks from sudden loud noises, rough handling, or any other disturbances during transport. If the ducks are exposed to loud noises, sudden jerky movements, or other stresses, they may become agitated, which can affect their health and meat quality. Handling the ducks gently and calmly will help minimize stress.

Humane Slaughtering Techniques And Considerations

Humane slaughtering of ducks is important not only for ethical reasons but also for the quality of the meat. When ducks experience stress during the slaughter process, it can negatively affect the texture, flavor, and overall quality of the meat. Therefore, using methods that minimize discomfort for the ducks is essential.

Humane Slaughtering Methods

The most humane way to slaughter ducks is to first stun them, which makes them unconscious, and then bleed them out. Stunning ensures that the duck does not experience pain or stress during the slaughter process. The stunning method that is most commonly used for ducks is electrical stunning.

Electrical Stunning works by passing an electrical current through the duck's head. This current renders the duck unconscious almost immediately, so it does not feel pain or distress when the subsequent steps, like bleeding, are performed. The stun should be effective enough to ensure that the duck is fully unconscious, and it should happen quickly to avoid unnecessary suffering.

Stunning is a key part of humane slaughter because it minimizes the duck's awareness and ability to feel pain. When done properly, it ensures that the duck is in a state of unconsciousness during the entire slaughter process, which is both ethical and beneficial for meat quality.

Bleeding the Duck

After the duck has been stunned and is unconscious, the next step is to bleed the duck. This is done by cutting the duck's jugular vein and carotid artery, which are located in the neck. Bleeding is important for two reasons. First, it ensures that the duck's body is properly drained of blood. Without proper bleeding, the meat can develop blood spots, which can make the meat less desirable in both appearance and taste. Blood spots in the meat can cause an unpleasant flavor and a tougher texture, so proper bleeding improves the quality of the final product.

Second, bleeding helps the duck's body go through the natural process of dying, which is part of the humane slaughter practice. It should be done quickly to ensure the duck does not suffer unnecessarily during this stage. The bleeding should be done by experienced personnel who can carry out the procedure cleanly and efficiently to avoid any delays or distress.

Handling During the Slaughter Process

While stunning and bleeding are the primary methods of humane slaughter, it is equally important to handle the duck gently throughout the entire process. Rough handling can cause unnecessary stress or injury, which can affect the quality of the meat. Ensuring that the duck is not subjected to sudden movements, loud noises, or other distressing experiences will help reduce stress.

After stunning, the duck should be handled carefully as it is bled and prepared for processing. The use of calm, consistent movements during the entire procedure will help minimize stress on the duck, which ultimately results in better meat quality. Ducks should not be left hanging or restrained for long periods, and any additional procedures should be performed as quickly and efficiently as possible.

Regulations and Alternatives

In some areas, there are specific regulations regarding the humane slaughter of ducks and other poultry. These regulations may vary depending on your location, so it is essential to check the local laws and guidelines before carrying out the slaughter process. Some regions may have specific rules about how ducks should be stunned, and there may be alternative methods of stunning or slaughter that are acceptable.

It's important to stay informed about the guidelines in your area to ensure that you are following the correct and ethical procedures. Some alternative methods may include the use of gas stunning, where ducks are exposed to a controlled mixture of gases to render them unconscious. However, electrical stunning remains the most common and widely accepted method.

Plucking, Eviscerating, And Cleaning: Step-By-Step Processing Guide

Once the duck has been slaughtered, the next steps are plucking, eviscerating, and cleaning. These processes are essential for preparing the duck meat, ensuring it remains clean, intact, and of the highest quality. Each step requires careful attention to detail to ensure the best results.

1. Plucking the Duck

The first step after slaughter is to remove the feathers from the duck. This is called plucking, and it can be done by hand or with a feather plucker machine. Hand plucking gives you more control, but it is time-consuming. If you have many ducks to process, a feather plucker machine can speed up the job.

To make the plucking easier, dip the duck in hot water (around 140°F or 60°C) for a few seconds before starting. The hot water softens the feathers and helps loosen them, making them easier to remove. Be sure to work carefully to remove all the feathers, including any pin feathers. Pin feathers are small, hard feathers that can be harder to pluck and are found under the skin. These should be removed thoroughly to ensure the duck looks clean and presentable.

If you are plucking by hand, start by pulling the feathers gently in the direction they grow. If using a machine, make sure to follow the manufacturer's instructions for best results.

2. Eviscerating the Duck

Once the feathers are removed, the next step is evisceration, which involves removing the internal organs. This is an important step to ensure the meat stays fresh and clean.

Start by making a small incision in the abdomen of the duck, just below the rib cage. This incision should be small to avoid damaging any internal organs. Be gentle when cutting around the vent (the duck's rear end), and work your way up toward the chest cavity. Make sure to use a sharp knife to avoid any tearing or mistakes.

As you cut, be careful not to puncture the intestines, bladder, or stomach. If these organs are punctured, waste material can leak into the body cavity, contaminating the meat. Once you have cut open the abdomen, carefully remove all the internal organs, including the intestines, liver, heart, and gizzard. You may want to keep the liver and gizzard for cooking or selling, but be sure to handle these organs carefully to prevent contamination.

After removing the larger organs, check for any remaining smaller parts, like the lungs or the trachea (windpipe), which may be stuck to the inside of the body cavity. Remove any remaining parts carefully to ensure the cavity is completely clean.

3. Cleaning the Duck

Once the evisceration is complete, it's time to clean the duck. This step is crucial to remove any remaining debris, blood, or waste that may have been left inside the body.

Rinse the duck thoroughly using cold water both inside and out. Make sure to clean the cavity well, removing any leftover blood, feathers, or other residue. This is essential for maintaining the cleanliness of the meat and preventing any bacterial contamination. If you notice any remaining feathers or debris, make sure to remove them completely.

It is also a good idea to check the carcass carefully for any damage that might have occurred during slaughter or evisceration. If you find any cuts or bruises, these should be trimmed away to ensure the meat remains of good quality.

Once you've thoroughly cleaned the duck, hang it up or place it on a clean surface to dry. Allow the carcass to air-dry for a little while before you store or package it. This step helps remove excess moisture, which can promote the growth of bacteria if not handled properly.

Final Steps: Packaging and Storing the Duck

After the duck has been plucked, eviscerated, and cleaned, it is now ready for storage or packaging. If you plan to sell or store the duck, ensure that it is kept at the right temperature to prevent spoilage. Ducks should be stored in a refrigerator or freezer, depending on how soon they will be used.

Make sure to package the duck carefully, using clean materials that will protect the meat during transport or storage. If you intend to sell the duck or its parts, make sure the packaging is labeled clearly with the necessary details about the product.

Handling, Storing, And Packaging Duck Meat For Freshness

After ducks have been processed, proper handling, storing, and packaging are crucial to keeping the meat fresh and maintaining its quality. These steps help prevent contamination and spoilage, ensuring the meat remains safe and tasty for consumption.

Handling the Duck Meat

Handling the processed duck meat correctly is one of the first steps in maintaining its freshness. It is essential to use clean hands or gloves when touching the meat to avoid transferring harmful bacteria. This is particularly important if you're processing multiple ducks or working with large quantities of meat.

Cleanliness is key in every step of the process. Make sure all surfaces, tools, and equipment (such as knives, tables, or cutting boards) are thoroughly sanitized between each processing step. This prevents the spread of bacteria or contaminants between different ducks and ensures the meat stays as fresh and safe as possible.

Additionally, keep your work area organized and as clean as possible. Wipe down surfaces regularly with a disinfectant and ensure that any utensils or equipment that come into contact with the meat are cleaned properly after use.

Storing the Duck Meat

Once the ducks are processed, storing them at the correct temperature is crucial to maintaining the meat's quality and safety. Refrigeration is the most effective way to store duck meat for short periods. The ideal storage temperature for fresh duck meat is 40°F (4°C) or lower. Keeping the meat at this temperature slows bacterial growth and helps preserve its freshness.

If you plan to sell the duck meat quickly, place it in a refrigerated display unit. This keeps the meat at the right temperature for customers and ensures that it stays fresh until it is sold.

For longer-term storage, the best option is to freeze the meat. Freezing preserves the quality of the duck for several months, but it's important to wrap the meat properly to avoid freezer burn, which can damage the texture and flavor.

To prevent freezer burn, wrap the ducks tightly in vacuum-sealed bags or plastic wrap. These methods keep air out and protect the meat from exposure to cold, dry air, which can dry it out and affect its taste. If you don't have a vacuum sealer, you can use regular plastic wrap to cover the meat tightly, and then place it in freezer bags to add an extra layer of protection. Be sure to label the packaging with the slaughter date so you know when the meat was processed, and always use it within a reasonable time frame.

Packaging the Duck Meat

Packaging is an important step when preparing duck meat for sale or distribution. Proper packaging not only helps keep the meat fresh but also ensures it stays free from contamination. Vacuum-sealing is the best packaging method for poultry. This method removes air from the packaging, which reduces the risk of bacterial growth and extends the meat's shelf life. Vacuum-sealed bags also help to preserve the meat's texture and flavor.

If vacuum sealing is not an option, wrap the ducks tightly in plastic wrap and then place them in freezer bags. This method helps to reduce air exposure and keeps the meat sealed from bacteria. For fresh ducks, the best approach is to store them in chilled cases or coolers. These should be kept at the right temperature to ensure that the meat stays fresh until it is sold or consumed.

Labeling and Storing for Sale

Proper labeling is essential when you are selling or distributing duck meat. The label should include important details like the slaughter date and whether the meat is fresh or frozen. This helps consumers know the freshness of the product and how long it can be safely stored.

If you are selling fresh ducks, they should be kept in chilled display cases or coolers to maintain the correct temperature. Make sure that the meat is not left out for extended periods to avoid raising the temperature, which could lead to spoilage.

Complying With Meat Processing And Food Safety Regulations

When processing ducks for commercial sale, it is essential to follow local meat processing and food safety regulations. These rules are put in place to protect consumers and ensure that the meat is safe to eat. Compliance with these regulations not only helps maintain high standards of food safety but also keeps your business legal and trustworthy.

Understanding Local Regulations

Local regulations can vary depending on where you are located, and it's important to know the specific rules that apply to duck processing in your area. In some regions, there are strict guidelines about how ducks should be slaughtered, processed, and stored. Some places may require you to process ducks in a licensed facility that has been inspected to meet specific health and safety standards. These licensed facilities have the equipment and systems needed to handle meat safely, minimizing the risk of contamination.

In other areas, it might be possible to process ducks on the farm. However, even in these cases, there are still rules you must follow. These rules could include the need for proper equipment, maintaining cleanliness, and keeping meat at the correct temperature. For example, you may need to ensure that the slaughtering area is sanitized and that you have a plan for keeping the meat cold during processing. It's important to get to know the regulations in your area and follow them carefully to avoid legal issues and make sure your meat is safe for consumers.

Complying with Food Safety Practices

Food safety is one of the most important aspects of processing meat. It's crucial to ensure that the meat stays safe from contamination and remains of high quality. Here are some key food safety practices you need to follow:

1. Hygiene and Cleanliness:

The first rule of food safety is to keep everything clean. All tools, equipment, and surfaces used in the processing of duck meat should be thoroughly sanitized before, during, and after use. This helps prevent harmful bacteria, such as Salmonella or E. coli, from contaminating the meat.

You should wash your hands regularly and wear gloves while handling the

CHAPTER 7

meat. This minimizes the risk of cross-contamination. Make sure to clean all surfaces, including tables, counters, and any other equipment that the meat will touch. This includes any knives, pluckers, or evisceration tools. Keeping everything clean and organized is essential to reducing the risk of contamination.

2. Preventing Cross-Contamination:

Cross-contamination happens when harmful bacteria from one source (like raw meat or dirty equipment) spread to another area. This can cause foodborne illness. To avoid this, make sure to separate raw duck meat from other food items. For example, don't store raw duck in the same area as ready-to-eat foods. Keep separate cutting boards for different types of food and clean them thoroughly between uses.

If you are working with large quantities of ducks, consider setting up a dedicated area for each step of the process, such as one area for slaughter, one for plucking, and another for eviscerating. This keeps everything organized and reduces the risk of spreading bacteria between stages.

3. Proper Temperature Control:

Temperature control is essential for food safety. Ducks should be kept at the correct temperature to ensure they remain fresh and safe to eat. If meat is stored at too high a temperature, bacteria can grow quickly, leading to spoilage or contamination.

After slaughtering, ducks should be kept refrigerated at 40°F (4°C) or lower. This slows bacterial growth and helps maintain freshness. If you are storing the ducks for a longer time, freezing them is the best option. However, ensure that they are wrapped properly to avoid freezer burn and to preserve quality. Always check that your refrigeration and freezing systems are working properly.

4. Proper Labeling:

Proper labeling is another important part of complying with regulations. After processing, duck meat should be labeled correctly. This label should include important information like the slaughter date, processing details, and any other health or safety information required by law. This ensures that consumers can trust the meat's safety and quality. Depending on your region, you might also need to include information about where the ducks were raised or specific details about the processing methods.

Chapter 8

MARKETING AND SELLING DUCK MEAT

Identifying Target Markets: Restaurants, Farmers' Markets, And Direct-To-Consumer Sales

When it comes to marketing duck meat, it's important to know your target market. Different customers have different needs and preferences, so understanding where your product is most likely to sell well is key. There are a few main sales channels that you can focus on: restaurants, farmers' markets, and direct-to-consumer sales.

1. Restaurants and Chefs

Restaurants, especially those that focus on high-quality or gourmet food, are a great market for duck meat. Many chefs prefer using locally sourced, fresh ingredients, and duck is a popular item in fine-dining menus. By offering duck, you can tap into a niche that many chefs are eager to fill with quality products.

To reach this market, you can start by building relationships with local chefs and restaurant owners. They are always on the lookout for new ingredients to add to their menus. One way to approach this is by offering a sample of your duck meat. This gives chefs the chance to taste the quality of your product, which is often the deciding factor when they choose a supplier. You can also provide information about how the ducks are raised and processed. Many chefs value knowing where their ingredients come from and how they are grown.

Additionally, you could consider establishing a regular delivery schedule. This makes it easier for restaurants to plan their menus and order consistently, creating a reliable supply chain. Once you've built up a relationship with local chefs, they may prefer to buy from you over large commercial suppliers, knowing they are supporting a local business that provides high-quality, fresh products.

2. Farmers' Markets

Farmers' markets are another great way to sell your duck meat directly to consumers. These markets are becoming more popular as people look for fresh, locally sourced food. Customers at farmers' markets often enjoy trying something different from the usual meats like chicken or beef, and duck can be an appealing option.

Selling at farmers' markets offers a chance to interact directly with customers, which can help build trust and loyalty. Many customers are interested in where their food comes from and how it is produced. You can explain how your ducks are raised, what they are fed, and how the meat is processed. Offering samples of your duck meat at the market is also a great way to attract attention and give potential buyers a taste of what you offer. This allows them to experience the quality of your product before making a purchase.

However, selling at farmers' markets does require a commitment of time and effort. Setting up and staffing your booth takes work, and you'll need to transport your products to and from the market. While this can be a good way to connect with local customers, it is important to factor in the time and energy it takes to manage a booth regularly. If you're willing to invest this time, farmers' markets can be a valuable sales channel for building brand recognition and customer loyalty.

3. Direct-to-Consumer Sales

Selling directly to consumers is another great way to reach customers. With the rise of online shopping, many consumers now prefer to buy their food through websites or social media platforms. By setting up your own website or using social media, you can promote your duck meat and expand your customer base beyond just your local area.

Direct-to-consumer sales allow you to build a closer relationship with your customers. People who buy directly from farms often care about where their food comes from, and they value knowing how it was produced. Through direct sales, you can share your story, explain your farming practices, and let customers feel more connected to your business. You can also offer home delivery or shipping services to make it more convenient for customers to buy from you.

This method also allows you to grow a loyal customer base. When customers are happy with your product and know they can rely on you for fresh, high-quality meat, they may return to buy from you regularly. Online platforms can also help you track your sales and gather feedback from customers, which can be helpful for improving your business and building customer satisfaction.

While selling directly to consumers can be more convenient for the customer, it does require an investment in marketing and customer service. You'll need to make sure your website is easy to use, and your social media profiles should be active and engaging. Setting up an efficient system for orders and deliveries is also important for providing good service.

Developing A Brand And Marketing Strategy For Duck Meat

Creating a strong brand is an important part of marketing your duck meat. A good brand helps set your product apart from others and builds trust with your customers. Your brand should reflect the special qualities of your duck meat, such as its local origins, high quality, and the care taken in farming it. Here's how you can develop your brand and marketing strategy to reach more customers.

1. Brand Identity

To create a strong brand, think about what makes your duck meat special. What sets your ducks apart from those raised by other farmers? For example, do you raise your ducks on pasture, or are they free-range? Do they have a specific diet, such as being fed grains or herbs that make the meat taste better? Are they treated with particular care, such as being raised in a stress-free environment? These details are important and can help you tell a compelling brand story.

Let's say your ducks are free-range, raised on fresh grass, and treated ethically. This could be a key part of your brand identity. You can use these details to appeal to customers who care about sustainability and ethical farming practices. Sharing your farming practices and the benefits of eating locally raised, humane duck meat helps build a connection with consumers who value these things.

Your brand message should be clear and authentic. You want customers to know exactly what they are buying, why it's special, and how it supports their values. If you offer a high-quality product that comes from a responsible farm, customers are more likely to choose your duck meat over others.

2. Packaging and Labeling

Packaging plays a big role in making your product attractive to customers. High-quality, well-designed packaging can make your duck meat stand out on store shelves or at farmers' markets. The packaging should be clean, easy to read, and show your brand clearly.

Include important information on the packaging, such as where the ducks are raised and how they were processed. If your ducks are free-range, grass-fed, or treated humanely, make sure these details are visible. Many consumers prefer to buy products that are ethically sourced, so highlighting this information can help build trust. You can also mention any certifications your farm may have, such as organic or humane treatment certifications, as these can reassure customers that your product meets high standards.

Make sure the label includes necessary details like the weight of the duck, its price, and cooking instructions. Customers need to know what they're buying and how to prepare it. Good packaging isn't just about making your product look appealing; it's also about providing the information that helps customers feel confident in their purchase.

3. Marketing Strategy

Your marketing strategy should combine both online and offline methods to reach the most people. Social media is one of the most powerful tools you can use to promote your duck meat and connect with potential customers. Platforms like Instagram, Facebook, and Twitter are great for sharing your brand story, showing off your ducks, and engaging with customers.

Start by posting pictures and videos that showcase your ducks and farm. Behind-the-scenes videos or photos of your ducks out in the pasture can help tell your story and make your product feel more personal. Sharing recipes, cooking tips, or ways to prepare duck meat can also encourage customers to try your product. The goal is to create engaging content that keeps your customers interested and excited about your product.

Social media is also a great way to share updates about your farm and product availability. For example, if you're going to sell at a local farmers' market or food festival, let your followers know. You can even use social media to announce special promotions or limited-time offers to create urgency and encourage customers to act quickly.

In addition to online efforts, consider attending local food-related events to promote your duck meat. Food festivals, farmers' markets, and tasting events are perfect opportunities to meet potential customers face-to-face, offer samples of your duck meat, and introduce people to your product. When customers get to taste your duck and learn more about your farming practices, they're more likely to make a purchase and tell others about your brand.

When you attend these events, make sure to have marketing materials available, like brochures or business cards, that share information about your farm, your ducks, and how customers can buy from you. These materials are helpful for people who want to learn more about your product after the event is over.

Pricing Strategies For Profitability And Competitive Advantage

Pricing your duck meat properly is crucial to your business's success. The right price ensures you cover your costs, remain competitive in the market, and still make a profit. There are several strategies you can use to set your prices, and each one helps you manage your costs while offering a fair value to your customers.

1. Cost-Based Pricing

The first step in pricing is to calculate your costs. This means you need to account for everything involved in raising, processing, and selling your ducks. Some of the costs you need to consider include:

- Feed: The cost of the food that your ducks eat.
- Labor: The cost of time and effort you or your employees spend caring for the ducks, processing the meat, and handling the business.
- Housing: Expenses related to housing and caring for the ducks, including any infrastructure or materials used.
- Processing: The costs involved in slaughtering, plucking, eviscerating, and packaging the ducks.
- Marketing and Distribution: The costs of advertising, attending farmers' markets, and delivering the meat to customers.

Once you've calculated all these expenses, you can add a profit margin on top. The profit margin is the extra amount that will give you income beyond your costs. It's important that this margin is enough to cover your overhead and leave you with money to reinvest into the business, whether for expanding, upgrading your facilities, or increasing your flock.

By calculating your costs and profit margin, you can ensure that your pricing covers your expenses and generates a reasonable income. This way, you are not losing money while running your business.

2. Competitive Pricing

Another way to set your prices is by researching the competition. Look at how much other farmers and producers are charging for similar products, especially other meats like chicken, turkey, or specialty meats like lamb. This helps you understand the price range customers are used to paying.

If you're selling at farmers' markets or to restaurants, it's essential to be aware of what your competitors are charging. If you price your duck meat too high, customers may go elsewhere, but if you price it too low, you might not make enough profit to sustain your business.

To stay competitive, you should try to price your ducks similarly to others in your area, but be careful. If your ducks are raised with higher standards, such as being organic, free-range, or treated with extra care, you may be able to charge a little more than others who are selling mass-produced products. Just make sure that the price reflects the quality and care that goes into your ducks.

It's important not to undercut yourself by setting prices too low. While you may get more customers initially, you'll struggle to cover your expenses and earn a sustainable income if your prices are too cheap.

3. Value-Based Pricing

Value-based pricing focuses on the benefits your ducks provide to your customers. If your ducks are raised using ethical, sustainable practices, are free from hormones and antibiotics, or are locally sourced, these qualities add value to your product. Many customers are willing to pay a bit more for meat that is raised with care and responsibility, and they often see the value in buying from a local farm.

For example, if your ducks are pasture-raised, free from antibiotics, and treated humanely, you can price them higher by emphasizing these values. Some consumers are willing to pay a premium for products that align with their values, such as supporting small farms or ensuring that the animals they eat are raised ethically.

Offering value-based pricing means you can justify higher prices based on the quality and ethical standards of your ducks. To encourage repeat business and bulk purchases, you can also offer discounts or bundles. For example, selling a whole duck at a discounted price when customers buy multiple ducks can help you attract more customers and build loyalty.

4. Balancing Pricing Strategies

It's important to balance these pricing strategies to ensure you're both competitive and profitable. Start by calculating your costs, then consider the market and the value your product offers. Set your prices to cover all your expenses while also appealing to your target customers. Remember that your price should reflect the quality and care you put into raising your ducks, and it should help build a strong, loyal customer base.

Navigating Local And Online Sales Channels

When it comes to selling duck meat, it's important to explore both local and online sales channels. Each type of sales channel has its own benefits, and by using both, you can reach more customers and grow your business.

Local Sales

Selling locally is a great way to build a strong presence in your community. By selling through local restaurants, farmers' markets, or grocery stores, you can connect directly with your customers and build lasting relationships. Many consumers value locally sourced food because they can trust that it is fresh and of high quality. Here are some local sales channels to consider:

• Restaurants: Selling duck meat to restaurants can provide a steady stream of income, especially if you focus on high-end restaurants that value locally sourced, gourmet ingredients. Many chefs look for fresh, unique ingredients to use in their menus, and duck meat can be a popular choice for fine dining. You can reach out to local chefs, offer them samples of your duck, and explain how your product is raised and processed. Establishing a regular delivery schedule can also make it easier for restaurants to order from you consistently.

• Farmers' Markets: Farmers' markets are a great place to sell directly to consumers. People who visit farmers' markets are often looking for fresh, locally grown food, and duck meat can stand out as an alternative to the more common meats like chicken or beef. At these markets, you can engage with customers, answer their questions about how your ducks are raised, and offer samples to showcase the quality of your product. While it may take more time and effort to set up a booth and manage sales, it offers a chance to build a loyal customer base in your local community.

• Local Grocery Stores: Some local grocery stores or butcher shops may be interested in carrying your duck meat. Reaching out to store owners and offering to supply them with your product can help increase your reach in the local market. This can be especially beneficial if you're looking to sell larger quantities of duck meat. Be sure to explain what makes your product unique, such as your farming practices or the quality of your ducks, to help differentiate your product from others on the market.

One of the biggest advantages of local sales is the ease of managing logistics. Since you're selling close to home, you can deliver products quickly and avoid the high costs associated with shipping. Plus, selling locally allows you to interact directly with your customers, receive immediate feedback, and build trust in your brand.

Online Sales

Selling duck meat online opens up a broader customer base and can help you reach people outside of your local area. With the increasing popularity of online shopping, consumers are more willing to purchase food products over the internet. Here are some key online sales channels to consider:

• Website: Setting up your own website is a great way to establish an online presence for your duck meat business. You can use your website to share details about your farming practices, provide product information, and offer customers an easy way to order directly from you. Make sure your website is easy to navigate and includes clear information about the products you sell, including the price, weight, and delivery options.

• E-commerce Platforms: If setting up your own website feels overwhelming, you can use established online platforms like Etsy, eBay, or Amazon to sell your duck meat. These platforms already have built-in customer bases, making it easier for you to reach people who are interested in food products. Be sure to include high-quality photos and detailed descriptions of your duck meat to attract potential buyers.

• Local Food Delivery Services: Many areas have online food delivery services that focus on locally sourced products. By partnering with these services, you can offer home delivery of your duck meat to a larger customer base. This option allows you to reach people who might not be able to visit a farmers' market or a local store but still want to purchase fresh, high-quality products.

Logistics and Regulations

While selling online offers a wider reach, it also comes with challenges. Shipping perishable products like duck meat requires careful planning to ensure that the meat arrives safely and remains fresh. You'll need to find a reliable shipping method that keeps your product at the proper temperature, whether through refrigerated shipping or using dry ice. You must also make sure you comply with any local food safety regulations related to shipping meat, such as labeling requirements and certification for handling food products.

Building Relationships With Customers, Retailers, And Chefs

Building strong relationships with your customers, retailers, and chefs is vital for the long-term success of your duck meat business. These relationships not only help you maintain a steady stream of sales but also foster customer loyalty, which can lead to repeat business and positive word-of-mouth recommendations. Here's how to build strong connections with each group:

Engaging with Customers

Creating a loyal customer base begins with making sure your customers feel connected to your business. One way to do this is by engaging with them directly through various channels:

• Social Media: Social media platforms like Instagram, Facebook, and Twitter offer an excellent opportunity to engage with customers. You can share pictures of your ducks, updates on your farm, and any special offers you have. Posting regularly and interacting with your followers through comments and messages helps build a sense of community. It also allows you to showcase your values, such as ethical farming practices, which can resonate with customers who care about where their food comes from.

• Email Newsletters: Building an email list can be a great way to keep in touch with your customers. Sending out regular newsletters with updates about your farm, special promotions, and new product offerings can keep your customers engaged. You can also use newsletters to share helpful tips, like recipes for cooking duck, or information about upcoming farmers' markets or local events where you will be selling your meat.

• In-Person Engagement: Selling at farmers' markets or through farm stands gives you the chance to speak with customers face-to-face. Engaging in friendly conversations, answering their questions, and offering sample tastings can help you build trust and encourage repeat purchases. You can also ask for feedback about your products, which not only shows that you care about their opinions but also helps you improve.

As you interact with customers, remember that building a community is key. The more your customers feel connected to you and your product, the more likely they are to return and recommend your meat to others.

Building Relationships with Retailers

If you sell your duck meat through local grocery stores, butcher shops, or other retailers, maintaining a strong, professional relationship with these businesses is important. Retailers act as middlemen who help get your product into the hands of more customers, so it's essential to foster a positive relationship with them:

• Deliver Consistently High-Quality Products: One of the most important things you can do for your relationships with retailers is to consistently provide them with high-quality duck meat. If your product is consistently good, retailers will be more likely to continue stocking your product and recommend it to their customers.

• Stay in Touch: Regular communication is key. Check in with store managers and retail buyers to ensure that they are happy with your product. It's a good idea to ask them if they need more stock or if there are any issues that need to be addressed. Maintaining a clear line of communication helps prevent misunderstandings and keeps your product front of mind.

• Offer Promotional Support: Many retailers will appreciate promotional support, such as special discounts, in-store demonstrations, or marketing materials that can help boost sales. Offering samples of your product or organizing tasting events at the store can also encourage customers to try your duck meat. The more proactive you are in helping retailers sell your product, the more likely they are to want to continue doing business with you.

Building Relationships with Chefs

Working with local chefs can be one of the most valuable ways to build your business. Chefs are influential in the food world and can introduce your duck meat to new customers by featuring it on their menus. To form strong partnerships with chefs, consider the following:

• Offer Unique Cuts or Specialty Items: Chefs are always looking for high-quality, unique ingredients to work with. By offering specialty cuts of duck, such as breasts, legs, or confit, you can provide chefs with something different that they can use in their dishes. If you raise your ducks with particular practices, such as free-range or organic methods, highlight these qualities to give chefs a unique selling point for their menu items.

• Be Responsive to Their Needs: Chefs have busy schedules and need suppliers they can rely on. If a chef requests a specific amount of duck meat or needs a particular cut, try to meet their needs as promptly as possible. Being flexible and responsive helps build trust and ensures that chefs feel confident in your ability to supply them with the products they need.

• Build Trust: Chefs value consistency, quality, and good communication. By establishing a reliable track record of supplying fresh, high-quality duck, you'll become a trusted supplier. This can lead to long-term relationships and steady orders. Chefs can also help promote your product to their customers, spreading the word about your duck meat to a broader audience.

By developing strong relationships with chefs, you not only create a reliable income stream but also gain valuable exposure for your brand in the restaurant community. A chef who loves your duck meat is likely to tell others, helping you build your reputation.

Chapter 9

FINANCIAL MANAGEMENT AND PROFITABILITY

Calculating Startup And Operational Costs

Starting a duck meat business requires understanding both the initial costs and the ongoing expenses involved in running your farm. These costs can vary based on the size of your operation, the location, and your farming methods. Breaking down these costs into startup and operational expenses will help you plan your budget, determine pricing, and understand how to achieve profitability.

Startup Costs

Startup costs are the expenses you need to pay before you can begin raising ducks and processing meat. Here are the main categories of startup costs:

1. Land:

If you don't already have land, buying or leasing property will likely be one of your biggest expenses. You'll need to consider the location carefully, making sure the land is suitable for raising ducks. Ducks need access to fresh water, good drainage, and enough space to roam. The property must also be accessible for deliveries and transport, and you may need to invest in land improvements, like fencing or water systems.

2. Ducks:

The cost of purchasing ducklings or adult ducks for breeding can vary. The price depends on the breed, how many ducks you plan to start with, and where you purchase them from. Hatcheries or breeders may have different prices based on the breed's popularity or quality. Additionally, you'll need to account for transportation costs if you are purchasing ducks from a distance.

3. Housing and Equipment:

Providing proper housing for your ducks is essential for their health and safety. This includes building coops, fencing, and water systems. Ducks need shelter to protect them from extreme weather conditions and predators. The cost of these structures can vary depending on the size of your farm and the materials used. You may also need other tools like feeders, waterers, and storage for feed. If you plan to process the ducks yourself, you'll need processing equipment, which may include slaughtering tools, plucking machines, and storage facilities.

4. Initial Feed and Supplies:

Ducks require a steady supply of feed to grow and produce meat. Initially, you'll need to buy feed for your ducks, as well as the necessary equipment for feeding them, such as troughs or automatic feeders. You'll also need bedding material for your ducks' housing, which should be changed regularly to maintain cleanliness and prevent illness.

5. Permits and Licenses:

Depending on where you are located, you may need specific permits or licenses to operate a farm and process meat. These can vary from region to region and may include agricultural, health, or food safety permits. Be sure to check local regulations to determine what permits are required and the associated fees.

Operational Costs

Once your farm is up and running, you'll have ongoing operational costs. These are the regular expenses that will keep your farm operational. Some of the main operational costs include:

1. Feed:

A large portion of your ongoing costs will be the feed for your ducks. Ducks need a well-balanced diet to grow quickly and stay healthy. This includes grains, proteins, vitamins, and minerals. The price of feed can fluctuate depending on availability and local market prices, but it will be a consistent expense throughout the year.

2. Labor:

If you're working alone, you'll need to consider how much of your time is dedicated to managing the farm. This includes feeding the ducks, cleaning their living areas, and processing the meat. If you hire employees, you'll need to pay wages. Labor costs should be factored into your overall budget to ensure that you can manage all tasks efficiently while maintaining profitability.

3. Utilities:

The day-to-day operations of your farm will require utilities like water, electricity, and fuel for equipment. Water is essential for drinking, cleaning, and any irrigation systems for growing feed. You'll also need electricity to power lights, fans, or refrigeration. Fuel is necessary for running tractors, trucks, or other machinery.

4. Healthcare:

Ducks need regular veterinary care to stay healthy, which is another ongoing cost. You'll need to budget for vaccinations, medications, and routine check-ups to prevent disease. Having a health plan in place, including emergency veterinary care, is essential to avoid unexpected costs and maintain a healthy flock.

Estimating Startup and Operational Costs

By adding up all of the startup and operational costs, you can get an idea of how much money you need to invest to start and maintain your duck farm. Knowing these costs will also help you set prices for your duck meat. You'll need to ensure that your prices cover both your startup and operational expenses while allowing for a reasonable profit margin.

It's important to factor in both fixed costs (such as land and equipment) and variable costs (such as feed and labor) in your financial planning. By estimating both your initial investments and ongoing costs, you can make more informed decisions about the size of your operation, pricing, and profitability.

Analyzing Feed, Labor, And Overhead Costs In Meat Duck Farming

When running a meat duck farm, it's essential to understand and manage three main costs that will affect the overall profitability of your business: feed, labor, and overhead. Each of these areas plays a key role in determining the cost of raising ducks and how efficiently your farm operates.

Feed Costs

Feed is one of the biggest expenses on a meat duck farm, especially since ducks consume a lot of food as they grow. Feed costs can vary based on the type and quality of the feed you use, as well as how long you raise the ducks before processing them for meat.

On average, feed accounts for about 50-70% of the total costs of running a duck farm. This makes it one of the most significant areas to manage carefully. To control feed costs, it's important to use high-quality feed that supports the ducks' growth and health. Choosing the right type of feed ensures that the ducks grow quickly and stay healthy, reducing the need for additional veterinary care or supplements.

You can also reduce feed waste by ensuring that the ducks are fed the right amount, and using efficient feeding systems to minimize spillage. Depending on your farm's size, you may also want to consider purchasing feed in bulk, as buying larger quantities often reduces the cost per unit. Additionally, making your own feed (if possible) or sourcing feed locally can help cut costs.

Labor Costs

Labor is another important cost to consider when running a duck farm. Labor costs can vary depending on the size of your farm and whether you do the work yourself or hire employees to help. Managing a small farm may allow you to handle most of the work on your own, especially if you are just starting out. Tasks include feeding the ducks, cleaning their living spaces, monitoring their health, and processing the ducks when they are ready for market.

However, as your farm grows and you raise more ducks, you may need to hire additional workers to help with tasks such as feeding, cleaning, processing, and handling sales. This can significantly increase your labor costs. Be sure to factor in the costs of hiring employees, including wages, benefits (if applicable), and any additional expenses such as training or safety equipment.

Even if you are operating a small farm, it's important to track your time carefully and calculate your labor costs. Sometimes, doing everything on your own may seem like a cost-saving option, but if the work becomes overwhelming, it may affect the quality of the ducks or the efficiency of your operations.

Overhead Costs

Overhead costs refer to the expenses required to keep the farm running, but which are not directly related to producing the ducks themselves. These are typically fixed and variable costs that support the overall operation. Common overhead costs include:

1. Utilities:

You will need electricity and water for various tasks on the farm, such as lighting, ventilation, and water for the ducks. The cost of utilities can vary based on the size of your farm, the type of equipment you use, and your location. Managing your energy use, such as using energy-efficient equipment, can help reduce overhead costs.

2. Insurance:

Insurance is another overhead cost. You'll need insurance to protect your business from potential risks, such as property damage, accidents, or loss of livestock. While insurance can seem like an additional expense, it is an important investment to safeguard your farm from unexpected situations.

3. Maintenance and Repairs:

Your farm's equipment, housing, and infrastructure need to be maintained regularly to keep everything running smoothly. This includes maintaining water systems, feeders, fencing, and any machinery used for processing or transportation. Routine maintenance can help prevent larger, more expensive repairs later on.

4. Transportation:

Transportation costs include the expenses involved in getting the ducks to market, whether that's delivering them to local stores, restaurants, or processing facilities. If you are selling directly to consumers or delivering to stores, transportation can add up, especially if your farm is located far from your target market.

Managing Feed, Labor, and Overhead Costs

Understanding these three key cost areas—feed, labor, and overhead—will help you run a more efficient and profitable farm. The goal is to balance these costs while ensuring the ducks are well taken care of, and you are providing a high-quality product to your customers.

To manage these costs effectively:

• Track all expenses: Keep careful records of feed purchases, labor hours, utility bills, and maintenance costs. This will help you identify areas where you can cut costs or increase efficiency.

• Invest in efficiency: Use feed-efficient systems, purchase in bulk, and maintain equipment well to reduce waste and repair costs. Streamline labor tasks with proper planning or by using automation where possible.

• Compare suppliers: Regularly review your feed suppliers, equipment providers, and utility costs to find the best deals without compromising quality.

Break-Even Analysis And Profitability Planning

When starting a duck farm, it's important to know how much you need to sell to cover your costs and begin making a profit. A break-even analysis is a key tool to help you understand this. It shows you the point where your income from selling ducks equals your total costs, meaning you are not making a profit yet, but you're not losing money either.

What is the Break-Even Point?

The break-even point is the amount of sales needed to cover all of your costs. Once you reach this point, any additional sales you make will result in a profit. To calculate your break-even point, you need to know your total fixed and variable costs and the price at which you plan to sell your ducks.

• Fixed Costs: These are expenses that stay the same, no matter how many ducks you raise or sell. Examples of fixed costs include:

i. Land Lease or Mortgage: The cost of leasing or owning the land where your ducks are raised.

ii. Insurance: The cost of insuring your farm and equipment.

iii. Utilities: Costs for water, electricity, and any other necessary services.

- Variable Costs: These costs change depending on how many ducks you raise. Examples include:

i. Feed: Ducks need food to grow, and the amount of feed you buy depends on how many ducks you have.

ii. Labor: If you hire workers, the more ducks you raise, the more labor you will need.

iii. Healthcare: The costs of vaccines, veterinary care, and any other health-related expenses.

How to Calculate the Break-Even Point

To calculate your break-even point, you need to add up all your fixed costs and variable costs. Then, figure out how much you plan to sell each duck for. Once you have these numbers, you can determine how many ducks you need to sell to cover all of your costs.

For example, let's say your fixed costs (land lease, insurance, utilities, etc.) amount to $2,000 per month. You also have variable costs, like feed and labor, that add up to $3,000 for the month. So, your total costs are $5,000. If you plan to sell each duck for $25, you can calculate the break-even point by dividing your total costs by the price per duck:

$5,000 ÷ $25 = 200 ducks

This means you would need to sell 200 ducks to cover your total costs. Once you sell 200 ducks, you will have covered your expenses, and anything beyond that will be profit.

Profitability Planning

Once you know your break-even point, you can start planning how to turn a profit. The goal is to sell enough ducks to cover your costs and then make money. Here are some strategies to help improve your profitability:

1. Increase Sales

To increase sales, consider ways to reach more customers and expand your market. You can:

- Sell at more locations: If you sell at a farmers' market, you could also try selling to local grocery stores or restaurants.

• Offer value-added products: You might want to sell other duck products, like eggs or specialty cuts of duck meat. These products can help bring in more revenue.

• Promote your farm: Use social media, a website, or local advertising to attract more customers. Telling your farm's story and highlighting your ethical farming practices can appeal to customers who value locally grown, high-quality food.

2. Reduce Costs

Cutting costs will also help you become more profitable. Here are some ways to reduce your expenses:

• Optimize feed usage: Feed is one of the biggest costs, so managing it efficiently is important. Avoid overfeeding your ducks and try to minimize waste.

• Use efficient labor: Streamline labor tasks by creating a schedule that maximizes productivity. Hiring part-time workers during peak seasons can also help reduce labor costs.

• Shop for better prices: Look for discounts or bulk deals on feed and other supplies. If you have a large farm, buying in bulk could save you money.

3. Increase Efficiency

Improving the efficiency of your operation can help you save money and increase profits. Consider:

• Investing in equipment: Automated feeders, water systems, or processing equipment can reduce labor costs and improve efficiency.

• Improve farm layout: Organize your farm in a way that minimizes the time and effort needed to care for the ducks. A well-planned layout can make feeding, cleaning, and collecting eggs or processing ducks much easier.

Financial Record-Keeping And Farm Accounting Practices

Running a successful duck farming business requires more than just raising ducks—it also involves managing your finances well. Proper record-keeping and accounting practices are essential to help you track your income, expenses, and overall financial health. By keeping good financial records, you can make informed decisions, avoid surprises, and ensure your farm stays profitable in the long run.

Tracking Expenses and Income

To manage your farm's finances effectively, it's important to keep detailed records of both income and expenses. This means recording every transaction related to your business. You should track:

• Income: This includes the money you make from selling ducks, duck products, or any other farm-related income (such as selling eggs or by-products).

• Expenses: Keep track of all the costs involved in running your farm. Some common expenses include:

i. Feed costs

ii. Equipment and supplies

iii. Labor and wages

iv. Utilities (water, electricity, etc.)

v. Housing and maintenance costs

To make this easier, you can use accounting software or spreadsheets. These tools allow you to organize your financial data in one place, which helps you keep a clear picture of how much you're earning and spending. If you're unsure about how to manage your farm's finances, you may want to hire an accountant who can keep everything in order. Having accurate records will help you understand if your business is making a profit, and it will also help you spot any financial issues early so you can address them quickly.

Cash Flow Management

Cash flow management is another key part of running a profitable farm. Cash flow refers to the movement of money in and out of your business. For example, money comes in when you sell your ducks or duck products, and it goes out when you buy feed, pay for labor, or maintain your equipment. It's important to track both your incoming and outgoing cash to ensure you can pay your bills and invest in growth.

In farming, cash flow can fluctuate based on seasons. For instance, during the growing season, you might spend more on feed as your ducks grow, but your income will rise when you start selling the processed ducks. Similarly, there may be times when you have lower income, such as during off-peak seasons or when you have fewer ducks for sale.

By carefully planning and forecasting your cash flow, you can avoid running into financial difficulties. It's a good idea to set aside extra funds during peak sales periods so you have enough money to cover expenses when income is lower. Having a clear understanding of your cash flow helps you make better financial decisions and keep your farm running smoothly.

Tax Considerations

Taxes are another important aspect of your farm's financial management. Keeping good records will help you track any tax-related expenses, such as those for farm equipment or any deductions you may qualify for. For example, some farmers can deduct the cost of feed, equipment, and other business-related expenses from their taxes.

Tax laws for farmers can vary depending on where you live, so it's important to be aware of any special tax rules for agricultural businesses. Consulting with a tax professional can help ensure you're following the law and taking advantage of any available tax breaks. A tax expert can also help you understand which expenses are tax-deductible and how to prepare for tax season.

In addition to keeping track of regular business expenses, you should also maintain records of any farm-related credits or grants that may apply to your business. This could include government programs that support sustainable farming or those that offer assistance for starting or growing a farm. A tax professional can help you identify these opportunities and ensure you get the financial benefits available to you.

Why Good Record-Keeping is Important

The main reason for keeping detailed financial records is to understand the financial health of your farm. By regularly reviewing your records, you can determine whether your farm is making a profit or if there are areas that need improvement. You can also see how much money you need to reinvest into the business to help it grow. Tracking your income and expenses will allow you to make better decisions about how to spend money, how much to charge for your ducks, and when to expand or reduce your operations.

Additionally, good financial records are crucial for planning the future of your farm. They can help you make informed decisions about whether you need to cut costs, raise prices, or explore new revenue streams. They can also help you secure loans or attract investors if you need financial support to grow your business.

Scaling Your Business: Expanding Flock Size And Increasing Efficiency

Once your duck farm is up and running smoothly, you may start thinking about ways to grow your business and increase your profits. This can involve expanding your flock size, improving your farm's efficiency, or even offering new products. However, scaling your business requires careful planning and investment to make sure the growth is sustainable and profitable.

Increasing Flock Size

One of the most straightforward ways to grow your farm is by increasing the number of ducks you raise. By expanding your flock, you can produce more ducks for sale, which means more income. Additionally, by raising more ducks, you can spread your fixed costs—like land, equipment, and facilities—over a larger number of birds. This can help reduce the cost per duck and improve profitability.

However, increasing flock size is not something to jump into without careful thought. Scaling up requires more feed, more space, and more labor. You will need to make sure you have the resources to support the larger flock, including the right amount of feed, water systems, housing, and staff (if you need additional help). Also, keep in mind that larger flocks may require more attention to health and management to ensure your ducks stay healthy and productive. Therefore, before expanding, it's important to assess whether you have the infrastructure, time, and resources to support the increased number of ducks.

Improving Efficiency

Another way to scale your business without simply increasing flock size is by improving the efficiency of your operations. The more efficient you are, the more ducks you can raise and process without a corresponding increase in costs. Improving efficiency can lower your operational expenses, which directly impacts your profitability.

There are many ways to improve efficiency on a duck farm. One option is to automate feeding and watering systems. By investing in automated systems, you can ensure that your ducks are fed and watered consistently without needing to manually distribute food and water multiple times a day. This saves time and labor costs, especially as your flock size increases.

Another area to improve efficiency is in the processing procedures. Streamlining the way you process ducks—whether it's through better equipment, more organized workflows, or more experienced staff—can help reduce the amount of time spent on each bird, ultimately allowing you to process more ducks in the same amount of time.

Optimizing your farm layout is also a key efficiency booster. The way you arrange your facilities, such as the placement of feed storage, housing, and processing areas, can reduce the time and effort needed for everyday tasks. For example, positioning the feed storage near the ducks' living area can make it easier to refill feeders, reducing unnecessary movement and labor.

By focusing on efficiency, you can lower your overall operational costs, which will allow for greater profitability even without increasing your flock size.

Diversification

As your farm grows and becomes more successful, you may also want to consider diversifying your offerings. Diversification means adding new products or services to your business to increase revenue and reduce risk.

For example, besides selling ducks, you can explore selling duck eggs, which are often in demand for their unique flavor and nutritional value. If you have a market for them, selling eggs can be a steady income stream that complements your duck meat sales. Additionally, you could sell duck feathers, which can be used for craft products or bedding materials, providing another potential income source.

Another idea for diversifying is to offer processed products, such as duck sausages, smoked duck, or duck pâté. These value-added products often have higher profit margins than fresh meat because they can be sold at a premium price. By offering processed products, you not only create additional revenue opportunities, but you also attract different customer segments who might prefer prepared or specialty products over fresh meat.

Considerations for Scaling

While increasing your flock size, improving efficiency, and diversifying are all great strategies for growth, it's important to ensure that you scale at a pace that works for your business. Growing too quickly can strain your resources and lead to challenges in managing your farm. Therefore, carefully evaluate each option for scaling and decide which is the most appropriate for your current situation.

You should also be prepared to invest in scaling efforts, whether that means buying more land, hiring additional staff, or purchasing new equipment. It's important to ensure that the investment required for growth will ultimately lead to greater profits in the long run.

10

Chapter 10

SUSTAINABLE AND ETHICAL MEAT DUCK FARMING PRACTICES

Implementing Sustainable Feeding And Grazing Practices

Sustainable meat duck farming is about adopting practices that protect the environment while still providing the necessary nutrition for your ducks. Ducks need a balanced diet to grow quickly and produce high-quality meat, but the way that food is provided can have a significant impact on the land and resources. By using sustainable feeding and grazing methods, you can reduce your farm's environmental footprint while also improving the health and well-being of your ducks.

Grazing

One of the most sustainable practices in duck farming is allowing ducks to graze on natural pastures or fields. Ducks are natural foragers, which means they enjoy eating plants, insects, and other food sources found in a pasture. Grazing allows ducks to get a part of their diet directly from the land, reducing the need for grain-based feed. Grain-based feeds are often produced through intensive farming practices that can harm the environment, such as the use of pesticides and heavy water use.

By allowing ducks to graze, you are also reducing the carbon footprint of your farm. Raising ducks on pasture cuts down on the need to transport feed over long distances, which helps save energy and reduce greenhouse gas emissions. Additionally, when ducks graze, they are actively helping to maintain the health of the pasture by eating plants and insects that might otherwise become overgrown. This means the pasture stays in good condition and can continue to be used for grazing without needing additional inputs like synthetic fertilizers.

Rotational Grazing

To maximize the benefits of grazing while protecting the land, you can practice rotational grazing. This method involves moving ducks between different areas of pasture rather than allowing them to stay in one area all the time. By rotating the ducks to fresh pasture, you give the grass and plants in each area a chance to recover and regrow before the ducks return. This approach helps prevent overgrazing, which can damage the soil and make it difficult for plants to regrow.

Rotational grazing is also beneficial for soil health. It helps maintain healthy, fertile soil by allowing natural processes to take place. For example, when ducks graze, they leave manure behind, which acts as a natural fertilizer, enriching the soil with nutrients. Rotating the grazing areas prevents any one area from becoming depleted and reduces the need for synthetic fertilizers, which can harm the environment and pollute water sources. Healthy soil also absorbs more water, helping to reduce erosion and improve water retention, which is good for the land and the surrounding environment.

Sustainable Feed Sourcing

While grazing is a great way to reduce feed costs and environmental impact, there will be times when you need to supplement the ducks' diet with additional feed. In these cases, it's important to source sustainable feed. Look for feed suppliers who offer non-GMO (genetically modified organism) and organic feed. This type of feed is produced without the use of harmful chemicals, synthetic pesticides, or genetically modified crops, making it better for the environment and the health of the ducks.

Choosing local feed suppliers is another key aspect of sustainability. By purchasing feed from nearby farmers, you reduce the environmental impact of transporting feed over long distances, which can contribute to greenhouse gas emissions. Supporting local farmers also helps build stronger, more sustainable agricultural systems within your community. This, in turn, can lead to better environmental practices, as local farmers are often more focused on sustainability than large industrial suppliers.

The Benefits of Sustainable Practices

Implementing sustainable feeding and grazing practices offers many benefits for both your farm and the environment. First, it helps improve the overall health and well-being of your ducks. Grazing allows ducks to eat a natural diet that supports their physical development, while rotational grazing ensures they always have access to fresh, healthy pasture.

Second, sustainable practices can reduce costs. Grazing on pasture reduces the amount of feed you need to buy, and rotational grazing can reduce the need for expensive synthetic fertilizers. By sourcing sustainable feed and supporting local farmers, you help build a resilient food system that benefits everyone, from the local economy to the environment.

Lastly, these practices help make your farm more environmentally friendly. They reduce the amount of waste and pollution produced, conserve water, and improve soil health. By choosing sustainable methods, you contribute to a healthier planet, which is essential for the future of farming.

Water Management: Reducing Waste And Ensuring Clean Water Access

Water is a vital resource in duck farming. Ducks need water not only for drinking but also for swimming and cleaning themselves. Effective water management ensures that your ducks have access to clean, fresh water while minimizing waste and reducing your farm's environmental impact. Proper water management practices help maintain the health of your ducks and reduce your water usage, making your farm more sustainable.

Reducing Water Waste

Ducks require water for drinking and bathing, and without proper management, water waste can become a significant issue. To avoid wasting water, one effective solution is to set up automatic waterers. These devices provide just the right amount of water for each duck, minimizing spillage and waste. Instead of ducks knocking over traditional water containers or spilling excess water, automatic waterers deliver water in a controlled, efficient way, reducing the amount of water that is wasted.

Another useful method to reduce water waste is installing rainwater harvesting systems. These systems capture rainwater from roofs or other surfaces and store it for later use. By collecting rainwater, you can reduce your reliance on municipal water supplies, lower your water costs, and lessen the impact of your farm on local water sources. Rainwater harvesting also helps ensure that your farm has access to water even during dry spells, providing a more sustainable water supply for your ducks.

Providing Clean Water

Keeping your ducks' water clean is one of the most important aspects of water management. Ducks are naturally messy, especially when they swim or bathe in their water. Dirty water can lead to health problems, including respiratory issues, infections, and other waterborne diseases. That's why it's essential to clean their water regularly and ensure that it remains fresh.

To keep your ducks' water clean, invest in cleanable and durable water containers. Choose waterers that are easy to wash and maintain. Automatic waterers, for example, can be cleaned regularly, ensuring that any leftover food or waste does not contaminate the water. Additionally, it's important to refresh the water frequently, changing it every day or as needed. This helps prevent the buildup of bacteria and keeps the ducks' water sources fresh and safe.

When setting up water systems for your ducks, ensure that you have a plan for regular cleaning of all water sources. By doing this, you can reduce the risk of diseases and health problems that may arise from contaminated water. Clean water contributes to the overall well-being of your ducks, ensuring they stay healthy and grow properly without the need for medications or veterinary care due to waterborne illnesses.

Water Recycling Systems

Another sustainable water management strategy is recycling. Recycling water helps reduce the amount of fresh water your farm needs, making your operation more resource-efficient. For example, water used to clean the ducks' living areas or to rinse off equipment can be filtered and treated before being reused for other purposes. This process reduces the amount of water that needs to be sourced from external suppliers and lowers your farm's overall water consumption.

Water used for irrigation is another area where recycling can be implemented. After being filtered, the water from cleaning tasks can be used to irrigate crops or pastures on your farm. This reduces the need to use fresh water for irrigation and helps conserve the water you do have. By using greywater recycling systems, which filter and treat water for reuse, you can make your farm more self-sufficient and environmentally friendly.

Implementing water recycling systems can also save money. Instead of purchasing large amounts of water from outside sources, you can reuse water that's already available on your farm. This not only cuts down on costs but also helps lower your farm's overall environmental impact.

The Benefits of Efficient Water Management

Efficient water management offers many benefits for your farm. It helps reduce water waste, which is important for both cost savings and environmental sustainability. Using automatic waterers and rainwater harvesting systems ensures that water is used efficiently and responsibly.

By providing clean, fresh water for your ducks, you also improve their health and well-being, reducing the need for veterinary care and improving their overall productivity. Clean water is essential for ducks to grow properly and produce high-quality meat.

Additionally, by recycling water for other uses, such as irrigation, you lower your reliance on external water sources and contribute to a more sustainable farm. Water recycling systems not only save water but also help reduce your overall costs by minimizing the need for fresh water.

CHAPTER 10

Waste Management And Manure Use For Soil Enrichment

Duck farming produces a lot of waste, particularly in the form of manure. While manure is often seen as a waste product, it can actually be a valuable resource if managed properly. Instead of letting it become a problem for your farm and the environment, you can use duck manure to improve your soil and reduce the need for chemical fertilizers. Here's how effective waste management and manure use can benefit both your farm and the environment.

Manure as Fertilizer

Duck manure is packed with nutrients like nitrogen, phosphorus, and potassium, all of which are essential for healthy soil. These nutrients are key ingredients in many chemical fertilizers, but using duck manure as a natural fertilizer is a more eco-friendly option. When used correctly, it can help enrich the soil, improving its structure and fertility without relying on synthetic fertilizers that can harm the environment.

By applying duck manure to your fields or gardens, you can boost the quality of your soil and support plant growth. For example, if you raise vegetables, flowers, or pasture grasses, spreading manure on your land will add essential nutrients, creating a healthy growing environment. This natural method of fertilizing helps improve the soil's ability to retain moisture and encourages strong root development in plants.

Composting

One of the best ways to manage duck manure is by composting it. Composting is a natural process that breaks down manure, along with other organic materials like straw, hay, or wood chips, into a rich, dark, crumbly substance that's perfect for enriching your soil. When you compost duck manure, you're not only managing waste efficiently, but you're also creating a high-quality, nutrient-rich fertilizer that can be used on your farm.

The composting process involves mixing the manure with carbon-rich materials like straw or sawdust. This helps balance the nitrogen levels in the manure and encourages the growth of microorganisms that break down the organic material. Composting also helps reduce odors and the risk of harmful pathogens, making it a safer and more environmentally friendly option than simply dumping manure in a pile.

Once the compost is fully broken down, it can be spread across your fields or gardens. The finished product will improve the soil structure, promote healthy plant growth, and help increase crop yields. Composting also helps recycle nutrients, reducing the need for additional chemical inputs, which can be costly and harmful to the environment.

Manure Management Systems

Effective manure management is crucial to prevent waste buildup and reduce environmental impact. Ducks produce a lot of manure, so it's important to have a plan in place for handling it. Without proper management, manure can accumulate and lead to contamination of local water sources, unpleasant odors, and other environmental issues.

One way to manage manure is by setting up designated composting areas on your farm. This ensures that manure is collected and processed in one location, making it easier to compost and reduce waste. These areas should be well-drained, so any liquid from the manure can be absorbed into the soil, preventing runoff. It's also important to keep the composting areas away from water sources to avoid contamination.

You should also regularly remove manure from the ducks' living spaces. Keeping the living areas clean will help prevent excessive manure buildup and improve the overall health of the ducks. For example, if you use a deep-litter system, regularly turning over the bedding and adding fresh materials can help manage waste and maintain a clean environment for your ducks.

Proper storage of manure is another important aspect of waste management. If you're not ready to compost or apply the manure right away, you'll need a proper storage system. This can be a covered bin or shed that keeps manure contained and prevents runoff. Always store manure in a dry, well-ventilated area to help it break down more efficiently and reduce odors.

Environmental Benefits

Using duck manure responsibly has several environmental benefits. By recycling the manure into compost, you can reduce the need for chemical fertilizers, which often have harmful side effects, like water pollution or soil degradation. Composting also helps to reduce greenhouse gas emissions since organic waste, when left unmanaged, can produce methane, a potent greenhouse gas. By composting, you're reducing methane emissions and creating a useful product at the same time.

Additionally, good manure management helps keep your farm cleaner and healthier. Preventing waste buildup in your ducks' living spaces and keeping manure out of water sources reduces the risk of contamination, promoting the overall health of your farm and the local ecosystem.

Animal Welfare And Ethical Standards For Meat Ducks

Animal welfare is an essential part of ethical meat duck farming. When raising ducks for meat, it is important to ensure that they are treated well and cared for in a way that supports both their physical and mental health. Ethical farming practices focus on providing ducks with a safe, comfortable environment where they can express natural behaviors and thrive. This not only benefits the ducks but also leads to higher-quality meat, which can be a selling point for your farm.

Free-Range and Pasture-Raised Systems

One of the best ways to improve the welfare of ducks is by allowing them to live in free-range or pasture-raised systems. In these systems, ducks are given access to large outdoor spaces where they can roam freely and engage in natural behaviors, such as foraging for food, swimming, and nesting. These behaviors are important for their physical and mental well-being.

Ducks that are allowed to free-range or have access to pasture are generally healthier and happier. This leads to higher-quality meat, which can often command a higher price in the market. Customers who care about animal welfare may be willing to pay a premium for meat from ducks raised in these ethical systems. While free-range and pasture-raised systems require more labor and management to maintain, they are highly valued for the improved quality of life they offer to the ducks.

Proper Housing

Not all duck farmers have the space or resources to implement free-range or pasture-raised systems. However, if you must house your ducks in a more confined space, it's still important to ensure that their housing meets ethical standards. Ducks should not be cramped or confined to tiny cages, as they need space to move around comfortably. Adequate space is essential for preventing stress and allowing them to perform natural behaviors like walking, resting, and socializing.

Ducks also need access to clean water at all times. This water should be clean enough for drinking and for swimming, as ducks naturally enjoy splashing around in water. Their housing should provide protection from harsh weather conditions such as extreme cold or heat. Additionally, it should keep the ducks safe from predators, which can be a concern if they are housed outside.

Good ventilation in duck housing is also important. Poor ventilation can lead to the buildup of harmful gases, which can make ducks sick. Keeping the housing clean and dry is essential to prevent the spread of disease and parasites. Regular cleaning and proper maintenance will ensure that the ducks stay healthy and comfortable in their environment.

Humane Handling and Processing

Ethical farming practices don't stop once the ducks are raised; they extend to how ducks are handled and processed. Humane handling and processing are crucial to ensure that the ducks are treated with dignity during their final moments. This includes using methods that minimize stress and suffering during slaughter.

There are specific ethical guidelines for processing ducks that help ensure their well-being. For example, following humane slaughtering methods, such as those outlined by organizations like the American Humane Association, can help reduce the pain and distress ducks experience during slaughter. Humane slaughter involves methods that render the duck unconscious before any further procedures are done, ensuring that they do not experience unnecessary suffering.

It's also important to ensure that the workers involved in the processing of ducks are trained in humane handling practices. This includes understanding how to handle ducks gently, avoid causing stress, and follow ethical procedures during slaughter. Creating a respectful and caring environment for both the animals and the people involved in the process is essential for maintaining high ethical standards.

Why Ethical Standards Matter

Raising ducks with a focus on animal welfare isn't just the right thing to do; it can also help your business. More and more consumers are looking for ethically raised meat, and they are willing to pay a higher price for products that come from farms that treat animals with care and respect. By focusing on humane practices, you can attract customers who value animal welfare and are looking for high-quality, responsibly raised meat.

Furthermore, ethical farming practices can lead to healthier animals and a more sustainable business in the long run. When ducks are raised in good conditions, they are less likely to get sick, which reduces the need for medications and veterinary care. They are also more likely to produce better meat, which can improve your farm's reputation and profitability.

Incorporating Eco-Friendly Practices In Farm Operations

Incorporating eco-friendly practices in your meat duck farm can help reduce its environmental impact and make your farm more sustainable. By making your farm operations more environmentally friendly, you not only contribute to the health of the planet but also create a more efficient and cost-effective business. These practices can help you save money, improve your farm's productivity, and appeal to customers who care about sustainability.

Energy Efficiency

One of the most important eco-friendly practices you can implement is improving energy efficiency. Energy is a significant cost for any farm, especially when it comes to powering equipment, lighting, heating, and cooling the duck housing. By using energy-efficient systems, you can lower your energy consumption and reduce your costs.

Investing in energy-efficient lighting, heating, and cooling systems for your duck housing can help keep your energy costs down. For example, using LED lights instead of traditional incandescent bulbs can reduce electricity use. Additionally, installing better insulation in duck housing can help regulate temperature, reducing the need for constant heating or cooling.

Another great way to reduce energy costs and decrease your reliance on non-renewable energy sources is by using solar panels or other renewable energy options. Solar panels can generate electricity for your farm operations, including powering lights, pumps, and other equipment. This can save you money over time and reduce your farm's carbon footprint, making it a win-win for both your business and the environment.

Waste Reduction

Reducing waste on your farm is another important eco-friendly practice. By looking for ways to reuse materials and minimize waste, you can significantly lower your environmental impact.

Managing manure is a key area for waste reduction, but there are other ways to reduce waste as well. For example, you can reuse materials for building and maintaining duck housing. Instead of buying new materials every time something breaks, consider repairing or repurposing old materials. This can help reduce your need for new resources and keep your costs low.

Packaging is another area where you can make eco-friendly changes. Instead of using plastic packaging or non-recyclable materials, look for packaging that is recyclable or compostable. Many packaging options are now available that are made from environmentally friendly materials, which can help reduce the amount of waste your farm produces. If you sell your duck products directly to consumers, consider offering reusable containers or encouraging customers to bring their own bags.

Biodiversity

Promoting biodiversity on your farm is another great way to make your operation more eco-friendly. Biodiversity refers to the variety of different plants, animals, and microorganisms that live in an environment. A farm that supports biodiversity is a healthier and more resilient ecosystem, which benefits both the environment and your farm's productivity.

Planting a variety of crops around your farm can help support biodiversity and improve soil health. For example, planting trees or shrubs along the edges of your pastures can create habitats for birds and insects. This can also help prevent soil erosion and improve water retention in the soil, leading to healthier crops and pastures.

Supporting wildlife habitats on your farm is another way to encourage biodiversity. Leaving areas of your farm undisturbed or creating small wetlands or ponds can provide a home for wildlife and beneficial insects, like pollinators. This can increase the resilience of your farm to pests and diseases, as these wildlife species help to control pest populations naturally.

In addition to improving your farm's ecosystem, promoting biodiversity can have long-term benefits for your farm's productivity. Healthy ecosystems are more resistant to diseases, pests, and extreme weather conditions, helping your farm remain strong even in tough times.

www.ingramcontent.com/pod-product-compliance
Lightning Source LLC
Chambersburg PA
CBHW071416210526
45465CB00001B/415